ERRATIC NORTH

ALSO BY MARK FRUTKIN

Fabrizio's Return (2006)

Slow Lightning (2001)

Iron Mountain (2001)

The Lion of Venice (1997)

In the Time of the Angry Queen (1993)

Acts of Light (1992)

Invading Tibet (1991)

Atmospheres Apollinaire (1988)

The Alchemy of Clouds (1985)

The Growing Dawn (1984)

a vietnam draft resister's
life in the canadian bush

ERRATIC NORTH

mark frutkin

DUNDURN PRESS
TORONTO

Copyright © 2008, Mark Frutkin

All rights reserved. No part of this publication may be reproduced, stored in a retrieval system, or transmitted in any form or by any means, electronic, mechanical, photocopying, recording, or otherwise (except for brief passages for purposes of review) without the prior permission of Dundurn Press. Permission to photocopy should be requested from Access Copyright.

Edited by Michael Carroll
Designed by Courtney Horner
Printed and bound in Canada by Webcom

Library and Archives Canada Cataloguing in Publication

Frutkin, Mark, 1948-
    Erratic north : a Vietnam draft resister's life in the Canadian bush / Mark Frutkin.

ISBN 978-1-55002-786-0

    I. Title.

PS8561.R84Z46 2008   C813'.54   C2008-900714-X

1 2 3 4 5   12 11 10 09 08

   Conseil des Arts   Canada Council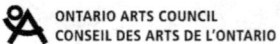
                     du Canada   for the Arts

We acknowledge the support of **The Canada Council for the Arts** and the **Ontario Arts Council** for our publishing program. We also acknowledge the financial support of the **Government of Canada** through the **Book Publishing Industry Development Program** and **The Association for the Export of Canadian Books**, and the **Government of Ontario** through the **Ontario Book Publishers Tax Credit** program, and the **Ontario Media Development Corporation**.

Care has been taken to trace the ownership of copyright material used in this book. The author and the publisher welcome any information enabling them to rectify any references or credits in subsequent editions.

J. Kirk Howard, President

Printed and bound in Canada.
Printed on recycled paper.
www.dundurn.com

Dundurn Press	Gazelle Book Services Limited	Dundurn Press
3 Church Street, Suite 500	White Cross Mills	2250 Military Road
Toronto, Ontario, Canada	High Town, Lancaster, England	Tonawanda, NY
M5E 1M2	LA1 4XS	U.S.A. 14150

To my parents

Contents

Acknowledgements 11

Part 1

1. Gatineau Hills, Quebec 15
2. Cleveland, Ohio 16
3. Simon 18
4. Louis 23
5. Contract 28
6. The Farm 30
7. The Cabin 33
8. The Swamp 35
9. Czar's Draft 37
10. Coming Home 40
11. Blackfly Season 41
12. Steve and Shirley 43
13. Soil and Stars 49

Part 2

1. Borisov on the Berezina 53
2. Winter 56
3. Bread 60
4. Conscription Crisis 63

5. Snow 67
6. Maple Sap 71
7. Poverty and Wealth 73
8. Teepee 75

Part 3
1. Civil War 81
2. Letterhead 83

Part 4
1. Wolf Lake: Spring 2004 93
2. Fire 102
3. Norman Morrison 105
4. Sweat 107
5. Apprenticeship 112
6. Numbers 114

Part 5
1. Fencelines and Potatoes 119
2. Water 121
3. Border Country 122
4. Hamburg to Boston 125

Part 6
1. Black Sheep 131
2. Orzo 136
3. Endocarditis 138
4. Vietnam Vet 140
5. Bear 143
6. Wood Thrush 148

Part 7
1. Cemetery: Autumn 2004 155
2. The Wall 158
3. Memory 160

Part 8
1. Circle 165
2. Wheels 169
3. Bust 175
4. Chagall's Cabin: September 2004 181
5. Portrait 183
6. Blue Log Cabin 185
7. Work 186

Part 9
1. Choices 193
2. Wilderness 195
3. Pumpkin 200
4. Books: Kafka and Melville 202

Part 10
1. Commune 207
2. Immigrant 211
3. Christmas, Duck 215
4. Wakefield 218
5. Earth 220
6. Spring 224
7. War Museum 226

Epilogue 229
Selected Sources 233

Erratic (adj.): (3.) in *geology*, stray masses of rock, foreign to the surrounding strata, that have been transported from their original site, apparently by glacial action.
— *Oxford English Dictionary*

Acknowledgements

MEMORY IS A SUBTLE and evanescent play of light inside the head. The critic Walter Benjamin once said, "Memory is not an instrument for exploring the past but its theatre," and the playwright Eugene Ionesco observed, "the light that memory lends to things is the palest light of all … I am not quite sure whether I am dreaming or remembering, whether I have lived my life or dreamed it."

Many of the people who appear in these pages will have different memories of certain events, will have seen those nuanced lights from angles other than the ones I have recorded. For any errors, oversights, misunderstandings, or lack of clarity in my recounting of events, I extend my most humble apologies in advance. Any mistakes are mine alone.

This book could not have been written without the hard work and dedication (and editorial assistance) of my oldest brother, Ren Frutkin, and his wife, Ann Berger Frutkin, who produced a monograph titled *Memories of a Cleveland Childhood*, based for the most part on conversations with our father, and presented to him on his ninetieth birthday. This monograph not only provided background information on Simon Frutkin and the Frutkin family, it saved me considerable research time and inspired my own interest in the subject.

Also, my deep appreciation to my parents, Rennie and Anabel, my sister, Marilyn, and my brother, Lawrence, for their help and encouragement. Thanks are also owed to Arnold Frutkin (my father's half-brother and Simon's youngest son), who provided notes for the monograph *Memories of a Cleveland Childhood*, as well as old photos of Simon, and answered numerous queries from his home in Virginia.

I would also like to thank everyone from the Wolf Lake Farm, and those formerly from the Farm, for their help and suggestions, especially

Erratic North

Steve, Shirley, Jochen and Monik, Colleen, Val, Fritz, and Paul. And special thanks to Val for the quotation from her short Farm memoir, *This Was How I Saw It*, and the story about Jochen and the trout.

Thanks also to Nicola Vulpe, Tom Henighan, Michael Carroll, Murray Wilson, Richard Taylor, and, especially, Faith Seltzer, my wife, for their readings and edits of the manuscript (or portions thereof) and their consistently incisive and helpful editorial comments.

Thanks, as well, to Hazel Mayer and Lou and Esther Seltzer.

And, finally, special thanks to Elliot Frutkin, my son, who, after hearing many of these stories at the supper table, suggested I write them down.

(Note: The chapter titled "Wheels" won first prize in the 2006 Duncan Campbell Scott Essay Contest.)

Part 1

Photo by Shirley Inget

1
Gatineau Hills, Quebec

I SIT IN A wooden chair at the kitchen table in a two-storey log house in western Quebec, about an hour's drive north of Ottawa. It's 1971. The cabin, facing south, rests on a slight rise at the end of a long valley that snakes through the Gatineau Hills. The hills, thick with pine, spruce, maple, oak, birch, and beech, are invisible because it is 4:00 a.m. — what the Japanese call the hour of the tiger — and the night is without a moon. Unable to sleep, I have risen from bed, lit a coal-oil lamp, and begun to read a book at the table in the centre of the kitchen. The silence is penetrating and deep, the kind of silence we no longer hear in the modern world with its constant cough of traffic and its white noise humming 24/7 from fridge and computer. There is no wind on this autumn night. If there were, the creaking of the square logs that form the cabin's walls would make the silence feel deeper still.

If you were to look in the kitchen window from outside, you would see I am alone. The single flame of the oil lamp pulses behind its glass globe. In the silence, my head bowed, I read the book before me. Kenneth Rexroth's collection of translations, *100 Poems from the Chinese*, rests in a pool of light on the table. The ancient Chinese believed that books embodied the power to ward off evil spirits. Outside the cabin, the night is lit with stars. It was Mohiddin ibn Arabi who first said: "The universe is an immense book." I recall those words as I lean into the light and begin reading, while imagining the vast empty sky arcing silently above.

Suddenly, I raise my head and listen. After a moment's confusion, I realize it's the sound of a horse-drawn wagon passing down the road. It's an incongruous, archaic sound that cracks open the silence of night. The wagon creaks along the dirt road at the foot of a steep hill, which magnifies the sound of the iron wheels.

I suspect it is Albert out there in the pre-dawn darkness, a Habitant bachelor who lives at the end of the road beyond a swamp. His small log cabin stands on a hill overlooking the nearby farming village of Duclos. The creaking of the wagon tells me he must be on his way to help out his brother, Louis, the French-Canadian farmer who sold me this house and farm. Several years before I arrived, Louis moved to a larger house — one with electricity — on the highway nearby. While I cannot see his houselights at night, Louis's fields and mine border each other.

The horse-drawn wagon rolling along the dirt road in the dark takes me back in time. Unlike a speeding automobile, the wagon takes several long minutes to pass. I pause to listen, my head raised from the book. The creaking sound, distinct against the background silence of night, returns me to a hundred years earlier when this log house was first built, returns me to the century before, when my grandfather, Simon, was preparing to leave his home in White Russia. It also takes me back to consider what I have in common with Simon and Louis

2
Cleveland, Ohio

A YEAR BEFORE, IN 1970, I sat with a dozen other young men in an office in a high-rise in downtown Cleveland, Ohio, waiting to take my physical for induction into the U.S. Army. On the far side of the world, U.S. troops had just entered a neutral Cambodia from Vietnam to hunt down Vietcong guerrillas. Richard Milhous Nixon, the thirty-seventh president of the United States, was in office. From a twelfth-floor window I stared out at the looming grey of Lake Erie. Canada lay directly across the water. I was already a Canadian landed immigrant, having lived there the previous summer. I had friends in Canada and even had family, on my mother's side, in Toronto.

Part 1

Fourteen names were called, and we filed into the examining room. The buzz-cut army doctor conducting the physical stood before me. This was my chance. I spoke just loud enough for him to hear. "I'm psychologically unfit for the military." His blank face and hard silence revealed that he had heard the same story a thousand times before from other naked young men. Ignoring my comment, he probed and prodded and tested, placed the cold steel of the stethoscope on my chest. He didn't warm it first like a family doctor would by rubbing it with his hand. He used this shiny metal instrument to determine the nature of my heart. I was already naked, and they wanted to go deeper still, inside, to listen.

What does he hear? Distant shelling? The staccato of machine-gun fire? Incoming rockets? No. Unaccountably, he hears the faint call of a whippoorwill, the trickle of a stream, a chaotic tattoo upon a drum.

I hoped at the time that he would hear an erratic beat, not an irregularity that was terminal, of course, but that somehow my heart would betray how it was clearly out of step with its fellows, that it did not beat to the same drum, that it did not march to the same music. I wanted him somehow to hear from the sound of my heart that I was one of those geological erratics, individual stones dropped by glaciers in the north country as they passed. A wanderer caught in great movements and abandoned at a seemingly random place when those movements, those glacier-like wars and political upheavals, melted away into nothingness. One can find erratics scattered across the northern lands, across the shield country of Ontario and Quebec and elsewhere in Canada. After a time, these loner stones begin to blend in; the moss and lichen that cover the native shield also cover them. Without a doubt, the needle of my compass was drawn, not by *magnetic* north but by *erratic* north.

But my heart beat happily away, with all the idiocy and steady tail wagging of a loyal dog. Although I had flat feet and was half an inch under the height limit, I passed as easily as a six-foot young buck with a killer instinct. The army was hungry. I would do.

A few years earlier, as a student at St. Ignatius High School run by Jesuits in Cleveland, I gave blood with my classmates for soldiers wounded in the early years of the Vietnam War. My Catholic-Jewish soon to be Buddhist-German-Russian-Irish-English-French blood now coursed through the veins, I imagined, of an injured American soldier. I was happy to do my part in restoring him to health but, at the same time, I imagined my blood trying to influence his views of the war, its "free radicals" breaking off and marching on him at the molecular level.

I, too, had marched — once. I was resolutely opposed to the war, and had even been a rather tepid, short-term, non-violent member of the Students for a Democratic Society (SDS), an activist group of the 1960s involved in numerous demonstrations, protests, and acts of resistance to the war. That one gathering, on the streets of Chicago, had cured me forever of marching. Being in a mass of people, whether a crowd of peaceniks or a division of soldiers, for some reason went against my nature.

Halfway through the march in Chicago, feeling distinctly uncomfortable, I turned down a side street and slipped away with a palpable sense of relief as the sounds grew distant, the megaphone-carrying leaders shouting, "Hell, no, we won't go!" and the crowd responding in kind.

Armies and protest are all about crowds. Canada, for me, was all about loneliness.

3

Simon

ALTHOUGH THIS IS ESSENTIALLY the story of one Vietnam-era draft resister and his "return to nature" in the bush country of western Quebec, it also touches on the stories of two other draft resisters in different places and different times. The first was Simon Frutkin, my grandfather, who at age eighteen fled his home in the Belarus province of Russia (known as White Russia) in 1896 to escape the czar's draft. The second was Louis Drouin, the Quebec farmer who sold me land when I first came to Canada in search of a new life and who resisted the draft in his own way during the Second World War.

———

Part 1

I was born and raised in Cleveland, Ohio, although I always add, "But my mother was Canadian, from Toronto." Actually, I was born in a suburb of Cleveland called Parma. No one I grew up with knew it was named after an Italian city, but everyone living in Parma claimed it was the fastest-growing suburb in the United States in the 1950s. My grade two class at St. Francis de Sales School had an unbelievable sixty children in it. Parma's quick expansion included an influx of Hungarians, refugees from the failed revolt against the Soviets in 1956. Parma was much like any other American suburb of the time. Each two-storey house of brick had a short, well-clipped front yard, a deep backyard with a barbecue, and a garage.

Cleveland the city, though, was another story. That's where my father was raised — in the heart of the city with the Irish and German immigrants. The near West Side of Cleveland was centred around St. Ignatius, a Jesuit high school, and St. Mary's Church, not far from the shores of the Cuyahoga River. My father, my eldest brother, and I all attended school at St. Ignatius, and my parents were married in St. Mary's.

It was a rough, tough world that my dad grew up in. One of his two maternal uncles, Albert, was a drunk who lived outside under bridges, and the other, Coonie, once had his internal organs jumbled when he was injured in a drunken fight with a detachment of local cops.

My father recalls, when he himself was eighteen, he went to the local bootlegger's house during Prohibition to buy a bottle of homemade booze. "I'm here to see Mrs. McGillicuddy," he said to the unfamiliar man who had opened the door. The man ushered him into the parlour where an Irish wake was in progress, Mrs. McGillicuddy laid out in her simple casket on the far side of the room. Unsure of what to do, my dad knelt, said a prayer, and left — without his bottle of hooch.

Cleveland is often the butt of jokes — it has been called the armpit of the universe, or worse. Poor Cleveland. Some of this reputation is well deserved. A surprising percentage of people who know nothing else about Cleveland know that the Cuyahoga River once caught fire. The river bisects the city with a slow-flowing stream of metallic sludge and polluted runoff from the steel mills that line the river valley. The river caught fire on June 23, 1969, flames shooting five storeys high.

The fire burned so hot it twisted railway tracks passing over it. At that time in Cleveland, most days the air smelled as if bad meat were being barbecued nearby.

I remember once driving along the freeway heading downtown and coming up over a rise on the expressway to see the Cuyahoga River valley spread out before me. It looked like Tolkien's Mordor — the sky glowed rust-red and dozens of towering steel mill chimneys flickered tongues of flame into the charred air. I guess business was good.

Before my father was born, his father, Simon, owned a tailor shop, Frutkin's Ladies Tailor, on the near West Side of Cleveland. He was a Jewish immigrant who, several years after coming to the United States, had married, started a family, and gone into the tailoring business. Two daughters and an infant son had filled out the family. The shop was a success. He had hired a girl who lived across the street to help out, an accomplished seamstress named Elizabeth. It was 1909. Elizabeth was twenty-one.

It had seemed like a normal day, like any other day. But, in an instant, the world can pause, and go spinning off in a new direction.

It is exactly noon. That moment when the shadows have dissolved back into the buildings, into the light posts, into the few thin elms along the sidewalk, but have not yet begun to bleed out the other side.

As Elizabeth crosses the street, she hears something unusual. A sound she has never before heard. In fact, she is not sure she has "heard" it at all — she may have "felt" it, trembling up out of the earth.

She has just left Simon Frutkin's Ladies Tailor where she works and is heading to her family's house for lunch. Before leaving, she had been watching Simon's infant son, Leonard, under the massive cutting table, filling and emptying a tin cup with remnants of cloth. In went the strips of cotton, silk, and wool, and out they came in a rush, dumped from the cup by his tiny hands. She noticed that he seemed supremely happy filling and emptying the little cup. She gazed at him with affection.

Next to her, Mrs. Frutkin, the owner's wife, was busy fitting a dress on Mrs. Kelly, a lady customer who stood atop the solid wooden table. Mrs.

Frutkin, her gaze focused on her own hands busy at the hem of the dress, had brought Elizabeth out of her reverie.

"Elizabeth. Elizabeth? Get me some more pins, please. And then you can go to lunch."

Elizabeth had retrieved the box of pins from the back room, saying hello to the family's other two daughters, three-year-old Hannah, and Rosalind, five, who were playing among the petticoats that hung from hangers in the hallway.

Then Elizabeth had left for lunch.

The moment hangs in endless suspension as Elizabeth, from the middle of the street, turns to look back. Not a breath of a breeze, sky the colour of milk.

It happens with a suddenness that seems surreal — and, after the pause, in an instant everything is moving again, only faster now, people running down the street, out of nearby houses and stores, trying to outrace their stunted shadows. But she notices the shadows cling to their feet.

Elizabeth rubs her eyes — how can something that is there one moment be gone in the next, leaving behind nothing but air, an open space? The sound she felt through the earth turned into the rumble of the brand-new Hankee Furniture Building, three storeys high, collapsing and crushing the one-storey dressmaker's shop next to it.

Already men are madly digging among the bricks and mortar, trying to uncover survivors. Elizabeth stands still in the middle of the street, unable to move, her legs gone liquid as if she, too, is collapsing.

The first body they drag out is Mrs. Kelly, followed by Mrs. Frutkin, both crushed to death. Elizabeth turns away from the twisted bodies, catching with the corner of her eye a flash of white at an elbow. A baby's cry makes her turn back. "He's all right!" one of the men shouts, reaching into the rubble and lifting a bawling Leonard out from under the sturdy table. He still clings to the tin cup. The man stands up and hands the baby to Elizabeth, the nearest woman available. She steps forward and takes him, holds him tight to her chest. He stops wailing, but she can feel him still shivering.

She squeezes him tighter as she sees, a few moments later, the broken bodies of the two little girls brought forward and laid on the sidewalk next to their mother.

At the back of the collapsed shop, where other men are digging furiously, a shout goes up.

A minute later Simon comes hurrying, limping, around the corner of the pile of rubble, holding his right arm with his left hand, blood trickling from his forehead. He sees his daughters and his wife laid out on the sidewalk, stops in disbelief, and collapses onto his knees, a breathy groan emptying his lungs. Elizabeth has never before seen such eyes, so wide open they seem all white. Simon places his left hand on his head as if afraid the top of his skull will fly off. A priest steps forward and squeezes Simon's shoulder.

Simon doesn't seem to notice but looks up. "Leonard? Where's the baby? Where's my son?"

"The baby's fine," says the priest. "You see, Elizabeth there has him.

Three years later the infant Elizabeth held was no longer my uncle but my newborn father. In the aftermath of the tragedy, Simon and Elizabeth had married — a Catholic and a Jew. She was a strong-willed young woman of character and independence of mind, able to resist considerable pressure from her own strict German Catholic family. She and Simon had been married in 1910 in a synagogue. Elizabeth was twenty-three while Simon was thirty-five.

In 1912 came a second child, a daughter, Fern. And then, a few years later, the couple separated. Simon fled to New York City to start a new life and a new family, taking Leonard with him and leaving Reynold and Fern behind with their mother. In 1921 Elizabeth died of post-operative pneumonia following a ruptured appendix, and my father and his little sister were left orphans at ages nine and seven. Following their mother's death, they were raised by their grandfather and step-grandmother.

My interest in Simon goes beyond the fact that he was my father's father and that my existence depends on the collapse of a building in Cleveland early in the twentieth century. My grandfather and I were both draft resisters in different places and different times. I never met him. He died in 1945, three years before I was born.

Part 1

4
Louis

On an autumn evening, I'm reading in the kitchen of my cabin where I live alone. I've finished dinner early. Out of the silence, someone shouts my name from the dirt road that passes through the Farm. I step out the front door of the cabin onto the large flat stone that serves as a stoop and look across the wide field. It's my neighbour, Louis, calling to me to come out. I take the long trek along a path that dips down from the cabin and crosses a creek that runs only in springtime, heading up toward the road where Louis stands with one of his older sons who has driven him over from his house for this visit. I've known Louis about a year. As I walk across the field toward the two figures in the distance, I have time to think about this man whose life has been so different than mine and yet similar in significant ways.

I first met Louis when I was searching for a farm to buy in the Gatineau Hills. With Jim and Tim, two Ohio friends, I was driving the back roads northwest of Wakefield, Quebec, in a bread truck converted to a camper in which we had come to Canada a few weeks before.

Jim was a tall, blond, all-American boy who had some serious unexposed cracks as a result of a year spent in Vietnam, while Tim was shy, quietly friendly, and dangerously thin. They had no interest in buying land themselves but were happy enough to drive through the Gatineau Hills with me while I looked. Along a dirt road about twelve miles from Wakefield, we sighted a hand-scrawled sign nailed to a fencepost: TERRAIN A VENDRE (lacking the accent). Jim pulled the bread truck over. We hopped down and walked to the farmhouse at the end of the lane.

The farmer came out from behind his barn — a massive, strapping lumberjack of a man in a flannel shirt and loose flannel pants held up by suspenders, the uniform of the local farmers even in summer. He exhibited the gruffness typical of people who had worked hard on the land for their entire lives. Looking as if he didn't suffer fools gladly, this Québécois Paul Bunyan seemed to embody the word *sober*.

Somehow the farmer got across to us with hand gestures and rough guttural French that the land he was selling was down the next side road and we could drive in and take a look. He didn't seem to care at all whether we were serious buyers. With hair hanging halfway down our backs and dressed in the scruffy uniforms of the day (jeans with no knees, torn and tie-dyed T-shirts), we probably appeared to him like people from another planet. He never cracked a smile, but simply pointed out the way and returned to his tasks. There was something profoundly simple and basic about him. Salt of the earth. The way he stood with his feet planted made us seem like excited jackals by contrast. I liked him immediately.

My friends and I took a look at the property and cabin and weren't impressed. Later we returned to our rented cottage on the Gatineau River near Wakefield, and I figured we had just spent another day of fruitless searching. But something was scratching at the back of my mind. The place we had seen — a lovely valley filled with wildflowers and surrounded by green, tree-covered hills — wouldn't leave me. We had rejected it out of hand because the cabin on the land didn't fit some preconceived, imaginary dream of a rambling, Ohio-style farmhouse we all had in our heads. But somehow I *knew*; deep inside I felt connected already. The land was pulling me. I was falling in love with the look of the place, the sturdy cabin, the sweep of the hills, the sweet summer air. After half a day, I suddenly realized it. Turning to Jim, I said, "You know what? We're crazy — that place was perfect!"

I was almost across the field in front of my cabin, still heading toward Louis and his son. As I came to the point where the path reached the road, I saw Louis was teetering, drunk. And when drunk, Louis was another man entirely, one who embodied the word *drunk*, inhabiting it as fully as he had embodied *sober* on other occasions.

His son, looking cowed, stood a few feet away, ready to catch him if he started to fall and prepared to pass a beer from the case of stubbies in the car when called upon.

"Mark! Mark!" he called. "Have a beer wit' me," he ordered.

There was no refusing this man, drunk or sober. He was larger than life, a force of nature. I took a beer from the son, who gazed at me with panic in his eyes. It was obvious he was having difficulty figuring out what his father saw in me — a hippie from faraway America who actually chose to live in this godforsaken land where winter lasted seven months and where the earth was more stones than soil. I drank my beer and chatted and then, as the evening was growing cool, Louis insisted I come over to his house to drink more beer in his kitchen. Climbing into the car, we took the five-minute trip, his son driving, Louis sitting in straight-backed silence next to him in front.

When we arrived at his house, Louis's son disappeared while we settled onto unpadded wooden chairs in the sparsely furnished kitchen. I glanced around: linoleum floor, a few glass Mason jars on the counter, a large cast-iron, wood-burning cookstove against one wall already pumping out heat against the chill of evening. In the corner, a deep cast-iron sink with a single tap.

We sat talking for half an hour while Louis chugged three more beers and lurched out the door to urinate off the side porch. He came back in and moved his chair before me, gabbing, leaning forward drunkenly, guzzling another beer, his sleeves rolled up. He was so drunk he fell kneeling before me, leaning one elbow onto my thigh. His wife, much younger than him, edged into the room and, in silence, gave us a fearful glance as she tossed two pieces of white birch into the stove and fled. Louis didn't look at her. His eyes were clouded, but he was excited, animated, there was something he had to get out, something he had to tell me that he considered of the utmost importance.

"You and me, me and you, da same," he said gustily, while gesturing with the stubby beer bottle.

"How? What do you mean?"

"No fight. No want fight war. Damn war. To hell, war."

There. He had said it. He drained his beer, staggered to his feet, took three steps across the kitchen, unbuttoned his trousers, and pissed in the sink.

One day in early spring, several years later, Albert Drouin, Louis's brother, told me the story of how Louis had resisted induction in his own way during the Second World War. As I was walking past Albert's cabin on my way to the village of Duclos, he had seen me and called me in. It would be the only time I was inside his place in the ten years I lived at the Farm.

His cabin still had plastic over the windows, meant to help defend against winter's blast. On this first warm day of spring, snow melting and dripping outside, newly awakened flies buzzed against the plastic on the inside. The cabin's kitchen was dark, except for a patch of opaque light from the lone window. The wood stove was emanating more heat than necessary. He gave me a cup of tea in a large chipped mug, and we talked.

Albert didn't have the gruffness, or the presence, of Louis, his older brother. He was something of a hermit, someone I would greet as he walked down the road on his jaunts to his brother's, a rifle over his shoulder in case of bears. Or sometimes he carried a shovel and an axe instead of the rifle. As he explained, he would wield the shovel to poke the bear in the belly and, if the bear didn't turn and run, the axe to whack him if he attacked. During bug season, he carried a small leafy branch of maple, which he flicked about his head in a futile attempt to keep away the blackflies and deer flies. With the maple switch whipping past his ears and across his back, he looked like a medieval flagellant trudging along the Via Dolorosa as he passed over the dirt road. In an entire year, I would see him three or four times.

During this springtime visit in Albert's cabin, he told me the story of their brush with Canada's military and their escape from the war. Like many French-speaking Quebeckers of their day, Albert and Louis considered the war to be a conflict between England and Germany alone, and not of interest to them. Why should they go far from home to defend the king of England? The mayor of Montreal went to jail rather than enforce a Canadian draft in Quebec, although I doubt that Louis and Albert had any idea what was brewing in politics in Montreal or Quebec City, or even on Parliament Hill, which was a little over an hour's drive away. In another sense, however, Ottawa might as well have been on the far side of the moon. It was an entirely different world, and the war was likely just a rumour they would hear about once a month in the village of Wolf Lake (Lac des Loups) at the Foran general store (English) or at the other store (French) run by the Beausoleil family.

Albert explained that during the war he and Louis had gone with a crew of other local men to work in northern Ontario to cut wood, their main occupation when not working the farm. They were to spend the night at a country hotel north of Sudbury with the rest of the crew and head up together to the bush camp the next morning. That evening the Royal Canadian Mounted Police and military police raided the hotel. The French-speaking draft evaders were arrested and taken to a jail in a nearby town.

"It wasn't such a bad jail," Albert explained, "but the window was a bit high."

The next day the French Canadians were taken to Toronto where they were held in buildings on the grounds of the Canadian National Exhibition. They were given physicals and most were inducted into the Canadian Army. But not Louis.

Albert explained: "When we were brought into this large building, an officer told everybody, one by one, to run all the way across the room. Each person ran when they were told. When it came to Louis's turn, he just shook his head. 'Non,' he said. He refused to budge. 'Non.' And he stood his ground. 'Come on. Run,' the officer urged him on, 'or we'll throw you in jail.' But Louis just stood there and refused."

I realized that was the moment Louis had become a draft resister. "What happened?" I asked Albert.

"Nothing. He never did run; but they found out we both had hernias and sent us home."

Lumberjacks with hernias. Probably fairly common in those days. Louis, it was clear, was not good at taking orders, would not make a compliant soldier. The brothers headed home to the Gatineau Hills, their war over before it began.

5
Contract

I bought the Farm in 1970 with Wally, a friend from the small Ohio town of Dover. I had met him in 1967 in Rome, Italy, while we attended a third-year-abroad program offered by Loyola University of Chicago where I was going to school. My older brother, Bud, ten years my senior, put up half the money for the Farm, and Wally and I provided the rest. We paid a total of $5,500 for approximately 200 acres, three log cabins in various states of disrepair, and a spacious barn with a shiny steel roof. I was to sign the contract at the notary's on behalf of Wally and my brother, as they were unavailable.

The notary's office was on rue Principale in the city of Hull (now called Gatineau), across the river from Ottawa. I told the notary that Louis, the farmer who was selling the property, advised me to bring cash to the meeting at the office where we were to gather to sign the papers.

"What?" the notary blurted into the phone. "I can't have you carrying that much cash into my office! I'll speak to him."

Apparently, Louis relented, for the meeting went on as planned and I was requested to bring a cheque.

On the appointed day, I joined the notary — a dapper, perfectly coifed Québécois in a black suit — in the boardroom where we awaited Louis. After a few minutes, Louis arrived with his wife, Maria, twenty-three years his junior (he hadn't married until well into his forties). They looked entirely out of place and uncomfortable in the well-appointed boardroom with its leather chairs and long mahogany table, as if the rustic couple from Grant Wood's painting *American Gothic* had stumbled into the lobby of a Hilton. Louis was dressed in a way that couldn't be called *out of* fashion because it had never been *in* fashion. He was a farmer and dressed in the farmer way — flannels and tweeds and little else. Clothes were for keeping warm or keeping dry; nothing else mattered.

Part 1

Louis sat to the left of the notary, Maria to his own left. I waited across the table from them. Louis never cracked a smile, barely acknowledged my presence. As I think back, I realize he may have been displeased with having to sell off the property that had been in his family for a hundred years, since the early days of Confederation.

The notary, the sleeves of his impeccable white shirt sticking out the appropriate half-inch beyond the sleeves of his black suit, went over the details of the deeds and the property in question — one full lot and two half lots, termed an "immovable" in Aldfield Township, County of Pontiac, Province of Quebec. To be exact, the property consisted of the southwest part of lots three and four and all of lot five in the first range, approximately 200 acres in all.

A Quebec deed of sale and contract is a thing to behold — there seems to be more interest in who is married to whom than in any other legal detail. Our deed of sale consisted of pages upon pages of previous contracts and deeds, all duly and importantly stamped by long-forgotten bureaucrats who had disappeared from the face of the earth, much to their own surprise, I am sure. Several of the documents held waxed stamps in red, one with a red ribbon affixed under the stamp. The documents included originals of earlier sales of the property, on fragile onionskin paper, to Louis from several of his relatives — Dame Pierre Drouin (his deceased brother's wife) in 1945, and Moise Drouin (an uncle) in 1944. The documents also included several death certificates from area churches.

I signed my name in three or four places, as indicated by the notary.

The notary slid the papers in front of Louis and handed him the pen. Louis took the pen in his palm, his wide worn hand that had cut trees with a bucksaw, turned soil with horse-pulled plows, slopped and slaughtered pigs, his broad hand that was not unlike a clump of springtime clay. He held the pen clumsily and stared at it in slight confusion. The notary reached out and gently positioned the pen in Louis's thick, stiff fingers. Without embarrassment Louis scratched his X.

I look at that X now on the last page of the contract dated May 14, 1971, as it appears between the typed words *Louis* and *Drouin*, with the word *his* typed above and *mark* typed below. In the centre of this nest of four words, Louis's mark resembles a plus sign (+) more than an *X*. An earlier document carries a similar + from Louis and a mark from the aforementioned Moise Drouin that resembles a Christian cross.

Louis made his *X*, I handed over the cheque, and that was it — we now had a farm, approximately 200 acres of rocks and trees, fields and swamps. But we didn't really own anything — when the land didn't belong to its own history, it belonged to winter (over the years I would see snow flying in every month, including June, July, and August), and when it didn't belong to winter, it belonged to the bugs — blackflies and mosquitoes — as we soon discovered.

6

The Farm

WE WERE AN ODD crew that headed out that first summer to live on the land: two couples, Steve and Shirley and Wilf and Isobel, as well as two singles, Wally and me.

Wally, with his cascade of thick black hair to his shoulders and his velvet-dark eyes, had the mad-monk look of an Alfred Jarry or a Rasputin married to the hypersensitivity of a Marcel Proust. What had he been doing in small-town Ohio with his all-consuming interests in Japanese gardens, philosophy, and drugs? He was definitely in the wrong place at the wrong time. Perhaps he was actually born in the wrong century, or at the wrong end of the century at least. With his huge round head and penetrating intelligence, I believe he could have carried on a credible conversation with Leon Trotsky, Leo Tolstoy, or Gustave Flaubert, and held his own. A true polymath intellectual, almost entirely self-taught, he didn't last long in the wild woods of western Quebec.

Wilf, a deeply intelligent civil servant with a Stalin moustache, and

Part 1

Isobel, a young suburban housewife distinctly out of her element, also soon found country communal living distasteful. After a month or so, they beat a hasty retreat with their nasty-tempered red setter bitch in tow, their nearly new van throwing up a cloud of dust as they disappeared down the road. A few weeks before they left, however, we noticed something odd happening among the domestic animals at the Farm.

Our menagerie included several cats and a drake in addition to the female setter. The drake, it was obvious, was in a constant state of sexual frenzy and bothered the setter bitch to no end, repeatedly cozying up to her for attention, nipping at her private parts, and making a thorough pest of himself in the name of love. The setter wanted none of it and spurned his attentions at every advance. But he was one persistent drake. Every time the poor dog sat down, whether inside the cabin or in the cleared area beside it where we had set up an outdoor cooking and sitting area, the drake, mad with desire, would be at her, rubbing his head and long neck along her flank, sniffing her, nibbling. She would put up with this for a few moments and then would snap at him and change her place, running ten paces away and again taking up her seat, looking proudly into the distance; whereupon the drake would again waddle over to her and pester away. This went on for several weeks. Two very small brains trying to come to terms with each other. (The bigger brains in residence, meanwhile, were having their own difficulties getting along.)

Finally, the day before Wilf and Isobel were to leave, perhaps the setter sensed their departure was imminent, or perhaps she had finally decided to give in to the inevitable. We were sitting around the firepit late on a sunny afternoon. At the edge of our outdoor living room where the yard descended into the larger field, the setter sat gazing down the valley to the horizon in the west. The drake came and sat next to her. He didn't pester, merely sat. For a while they rested peacefully side by side, both staring straight ahead. As we watched in silent amazement, the setter slowly raised her left front leg and draped it around the drake's shoulder (if drakes can be said to have shoulders) as if to embrace him. They sat, quite pleased with themselves, the sad end to a romance doomed from the start.

The other couple who moved out with us to the Farm that summer was Steve and Shirley, visual artists I had met in Toronto on my arrival in Canada when I lived there for several months. They had been attending the Ontario College of Art and renting a huge old three-storey house rife with cockroaches on Dundas Street in Chinatown just around the corner from the Art Gallery of Ontario. The house was filled with artists of all sorts, intellectuals, and students, and was a constant vortex of creative energy, volatile emotional displays, and often futile attempts to garner money, food, drink, and/or drugs of various kinds.

Steve and Shirley were more down to earth than many of the other artists living in the house. When we got to the country, it turned out that they were the only ones who were actually skilled at starting a fire or handling an axe (except for French-Canadian Wilf), essential skills for life in the bush.

I eventually learned how to use an axe, of course. Ten years in a cabin with no electricity and no running water, heated exclusively with wood — if I hadn't learned, I would have been found frozen in my bed at the end of the first winter.

―――――

An axe is a simple-minded tool, one that hasn't changed substantially in several thousand years. I love the way the handle curves sweetly to resolve itself into the weighted head of a bird of prey, the way the handle feels in the palms, this singular extension of the arms with its bludgeon weight at the end, not balanced at all but throwing out its power and force and strength so it can come crashing down on the ash or maple log, splitting it perfectly in two. The axe handle is made from the same material as it cuts, its supple curve like the leg of an animal, a bit of stream caught in its wandering. And that head, that heavy thoughtless head (the skull of a medieval peasant asleep), made of steel sharpened to a splitting edge to blow the world in two.

Part 1

7
The Cabin

The cabin itself was a beautiful, functional structure that had stood over a hundred years on its small rise at the end of the valley, surrounded by three huge lilac bushes, twenty feet across, the size and shape of Mongolian yurts. Past the cabin and beyond the rise, a cedar swamp started fifty feet from the back door. A century before, towering cedars, bent like bows rising out of the earth, had been cut from that swamp, stripped of leaves and branches, dragged up to the house site and prepared. The first owners had squared the logs using an adze — the adze cuts were still visible every eight inches or so on the log's face, which gave the surface a rough scalloped finish. Next, they would cut the ends for mortising. At the corners of the two-storey cabin, the fits were all different — and perfect. People who have torn down log cabins find it impossible to pull apart these joints. The logs must be unstacked one by one, as they were laid.

The cabin's outside dimensions were exactly twenty-four by twenty feet. A solid structure — the timbers in its walls were each about one foot square. After a hundred years it still stood unwavering against demons of wind and weather. The cedar wood, which had gained a patina of greys, blacks, tans, and pale yellows over the years, was anathema to insects. With cement chinking between the logs and tongue-in-groove panelling on the inside, it proved a bulwark against long Quebec winters, rainy springs, stormy hot summers, and any other battering nature could dish out. The steeply sloping roof would have to be replaced every so many years, but otherwise the house was put in place and held. Not quite timeless but longer lasting than any of its fickle residents.

The front door of the cabin was in the middle of the south-facing wall. One stepped up from a large flat piece of grey granite that served as a doorstep and entered the kitchen, a single room on the left running to the back of the house. Another single open room was situated on the right, with one window in the south wall and two in the east. The panes in these windows had the imperfections and ripples found in antique glass. Inside, the cabin was dark, cave-like, especially the kitchen, which had but one window, in the west wall. There was no window in the front door, or the rear, which led out the back of the kitchen. Eventually, I added an attached back shed for tools, a second lean-to shed ten steps out the back door for storing cordwood, and an outhouse thirty feet down the path, with the words ABSOLUTE COMFORT painted in large blue letters on its side.

That first summer, however, before the outhouse made its appearance, our privy consisted of a plastic toilet seat hung by ropes from a tripod of poles arranged over a hastily dug pit — its weird combination of modern technology and basic earthiness somehow appropriate for the time and place and another sure sign that we were indeed back-to-the-land hippies. (In later years we learned that the best toilet seat for an outhouse was a piece of Styrofoam with a hole cut in the middle. Even at minus thirty-five degrees, it heated up immediately on contact with the skin of gluteus maximus. It proved far superior to plastic or wood in freezing weather.)

Back inside the cabin, a thin wall of tongue-in-groove vertical maple boards divided the kitchen from the sitting room. The yellow-painted ceilings were heavily smoke-stained. The floor, meanwhile, was certainly a most extraordinary and unusual testament to time. Slats of tongue-in-groove maple (or perhaps pine; it was hard to tell due to aging) were so worn in places, in front of the wood stove, for example, that the knots in the wood stood up a full three-quarters of an inch from the softer wood around them. I don't know if this was the original floor of the house, but I suspect, with that amount of wear, it must have been.

The cabin felt profoundly warm, earthy, timeless, and sad. Before my arrival on the premises, an old Irish woman, a relative of Louis's named Mrs. Pierre Drouin, had lived here alone for nine years, her only companions a bushy collection of indoor plants. She was always known by her husband's name, even though she outlived him by years. No one I knew could remember her real name.

In the end, I, too, stayed just over nine years in the cabin. I wasn't always alone, but there were many long periods when solitude was my normal condition. The loneliness I experienced then was not one steeped in self-pity and melancholy. It was a loneliness that held a touch of sadness as well as a touch of delight. At times my closest companion was my dog, Fletcher Goodfellow, a mix of collie and husky, black and tan, with a soft silky ruff around his neck. He was long and rangy, with a sizable snout, and was completely devoted to me.

Like any rural dweller, I had a few cats, as well. One autumn, when two females gave birth at the same time, I was suddenly the proud owner of thirteen felines — far too many for one small cabin. I managed to give away most of the kittens, although two, when half-grown, were killed in midwinter by an owl on the path behind the house.

For companionship I also had the song of the whippoorwill out the back door on summer evenings and, out front, more stars than I have ever before encountered. A clear view of the magnificent dust of the Milky Way was mine any time of year.

8

The Swamp

ONE DAY I TAKE a walk into the swamp behind the cabin. In dry weather it is possible to explore its innumerable tangled mysteries. For reckoning one has the mountain to the west and a towering, sixty-foot-high, dead, barkless elm tree in the swamp's heart. The cedar forest, which covers about a third of the swamp, runs right up to the base of the mountain. I use the term *mountain* loosely — these are high, tree-thick hills. The Laurentian chain, with the Gatineaus at their southwestern end, are some of the world's oldest mountains. They feel old — covered in loose rock, granite and quartz, their cragginess softened by the thickness of the pine and maple that cover them, as well as the thin stands of oak on the heights.

The cedar swamp behind the cabin feels ancient, like something out of a Grimm's fairy tale, telling of a time when Europe, too, was a forest of shadows. The old white cedars, *arbor vitae* in Latin, don't attain a great height, but some of these are two to three feet in diameter, with a distinct bend to the trunk. The ground here is soft and covered in thick moss and pocked with numerous pools and humps. In the evening, with the sun slanting through the forest, they are indeed "cedar lands aflame with gold light," as Ottawa's most famous poet, Archibald Lampman, wrote in 1895.

As I explore the swamp alone, wandering with no distinct purpose, I slowly become aware of a peculiar sensation — I am lost. Somehow the high hill to the west is out of sight, the towering dead elm at the swamp's centre is hidden from me, and I'm struggling through a tangle of bush and grass, weed and stunted tree. In the midst of this chaos, I realize there is no possibility that I can begin to retrace my steps.

I hear a dog barking in the distance. Turning my head, I listen.

Could that be the sound of the czar's troops coming for me, searching for the young man missing from the town of Borisov, who has gone into the forest to escape Russia, to leave his home forever, or die trying?

My name is Simon. I wander through this swamp, trying to escape, lost. I am the tenth child in a family of eleven. My father, Lazar, died when I was young, and my mother has done all she could to raise us well, with the help of the Jewish community. I have lived in Borisov all my life, the second city in the province of Minsk, in the country called Belarus. I was a meshchane, *a town dweller, not a* zemledel'tsy, *one who works the land. I have always been hungry. Once, as a child, I told my mother I met the doctor on the street. He said I looked thin and should have more potatoes. My worried mother contacted the doctor — he said he didn't even know who I was.*

I attended the cheder, *or Hebrew school, where I felt the masters were sadistic, cruel, and bigoted. It will leave me with a lifelong distaste for religion. I am eighteen years old, and it is time to leave or the army will get me. With my brother, Samuel, I have been walking and hitching wagons to the border with Germany. We have been hiking for days through forests, fields, and swamps. We will slip across the border at night and head to Hamburg where we will buy steerage passage on a ship to*

America for the equivalent of $30 — to the city of Boston, and then on to Cleveland where other Jewish immigrants from my city have gone and will help us. It is the Jewish year 5656 (1896 to the Christians) — I will never serve in the czar's army. Never.

Again, I hear a dog barking in the distance. I am lost in a swamp. Perhaps this is good — good that I am lost at this moment. Perhaps I am so lost the czar's soldiers can never find me in this swamp. Perhaps I am so lost I am invisible.

I walk on through the tangle of brush, low trees, vines that trip me up. I try to be silent, but I am sure they can hear the sound of my breathing, the sound my feet make as they crush small sticks and plants. I can hear the dogs coming closer now. Excited, they bark more insistently. I hurry on, not knowing the direction, away from the sound of the dogs.

It is growing dark. Through the trees I see a cabin, a log cabin, not too far off. A thin tail of smoke from the chimney wavers into the sky. I recognize it. Home.

9
Czar's Draft

MOST OF THE JEWS of Russia in the nineteenth century were restricted by imperial decree to living in certain regions called the Pale of Settlement, where they struggled in dire poverty. In 1880, four million of the world's 7.7 million Jews lived in the Pale in twenty-five provinces, including Lithuania, Ukraine, Byelorussia, Crimea, and part of Poland. Numerous restrictions on professions and trade ensured the Pale was an "economic Siberia."

The czar's draft, especially under Nicholas I (1825–55), was widely used to try to break the Jews away from their religion. Each village was to supply a required number of male recruits between the ages of eight and twenty-five for twenty-five years of service. To fill the quotas, children were sometimes kidnapped, taken for re-education, and forced to convert to Christianity.

Simon decided to leave because he had heard stories about the czar's army. The memories of that horrific time under Nicholas I were still fresh. During that period, Jews had to provide four times as many recruits as all other Russian subjects. Half the children, taken from their families and raised in barracks, died before they turned eighteen, the age at which they were expected to join a regiment. The *shtetls*, or villages, in the countryside, and some of the towns, too, were filled with nothing but old men, women, and young children. In St. Petersburg, Jewish boys were forced into hot baths and thence immediately into ice holes in the river in order to try to convert them before they entered the army. They were driven back and forth until they were "saved," or died from drowning, or their hearts gave out. And once, at a place called Orel, on a bitter winter night, more than a hundred little boys were taken to town on sledges, but on arrival they were found frozen to death.

Under Czar Nicholas, young Jewish men who wanted to stay home found a variety of ways to avoid the draft. Self-mutilation was common. Boys went on year-long fasts, and "experts" were hired to render them unfit for service by puncturing their eardrums, temporarily paralyzing hands, or even removing an eye. Eventually, the government introduced a regulation that stated that the families of sons who had rendered themselves unfit for service had to provide two recruits for the army instead of one, and this second one only counted as one-third for the totals required of the community. Fraudulent adoptions to gain "only son" exemptions were common, as was the committing of crimes to obtain "bad character" disqualifications. Others avoided the draft by their relations claiming they were dead.

A particularly insidious decree passed under Nicholas stated that any Jew without valid papers (whether lost, stolen, expired, or confiscated by the government itself) could be reported to the army office, which then demanded his appearance as a recruit. In these cases the informer received a recruitment exemption for a member of his own family. As Mary Antin observed in *The Promised Land*, "There were men in Polotzk (in Belarus) whose faces made you old in a minute. They had served under Nicholas I...."

The draft was not the only pressure driving Jews to emigrate. Widespread poverty, hunger, and disease, and the hope for a new life were significant causes of increasing emigration. From 1820 to 1870, only 7,500 Jews emigrated from Russia to the United States. In the next ten years (1871–80), 40,000 emigrated. From 1881 to 1890, the number more than tripled to 135,000. During the next twenty years, from 1890 to 1910, following further pogroms in Russia in 1891, an astounding one million Jews immigrated to the United States.

During this last period, Jews in the Pale were told they could no longer live within fifty *versts* (about thirty-three miles) of the border. If they lived any closer to the border, it was too easy for them to disappear over it. Also, the authorities hoped to curtail smuggling, which was rampant and difficult to control.

Under Czar Alexander II (1855–1881), the serfs were freed and there occurred a brief "spring" in the treatment of Jews. The draft was shortened from twenty-five years to fifteen and eventually to five years, but there was always the fear among Jews that the old draft rules would be reinstated. Alexander II was assassinated in 1881, and pogroms against the Jews immediately followed. Alexander III (1881–1894) then instituted another path of reform beginning later in 1881.

In 1888, however, Alexander III and his family were involved in a railway accident. Although the czar and his family survived, his spiritual adviser interpreted the accident as a sign from heaven to turn away from his path of reform. The czar took the advice, and more pogroms against the Jews ensued.

One can easily see why my grandfather and other young men wanted to leave Russia: the persistent recurring pogroms, the czar's draft, the poverty, the pain and suffering endured for simply being Jewish. A list of draft evaders from the Borisov district, dated December 27, 1880, includes the names of 163 young men. The lure of the golden streets of America was irresistible.

10
Coming Home

DURING THE VIETNAM WAR era, thousands of young American men were moving to Canada or Sweden to avoid the U.S. draft. As a college student at Loyola University in Chicago, I often discussed the war deep into the night with my roommates and other students. We believed that the war was wrong, ill considered, and hypocritical. We distrusted the domino theory, which posited that if Vietnam went communist then numerous other countries in the region and around the world would follow suit, like dominoes tumbling over. Ultimately, the theory proved to be a fallacy.

Four out of the five students I lived with in my senior year at Loyola University in Chicago left the United States to come to Canada. The war was the apparent reason, but there were other factors, as well.

For our third year of university, the five of us had all attended the Loyola University campus in Rome, Italy, living in the area called Monte Mario, some distance from the heart of the city. Our dormitory and classrooms were located in a single five-storey building at the end of a long tree-lined drive, a former residence of the Swiss Guard, the soldiers of the pope. From the roof of the building one could look out over the hills of Rome in the distance.

After travelling for the better part of a year throughout Italy and Europe, and being introduced to the refinements of European culture and art (not to mention food and wine), we returned in late summer to Loyola University in Chicago. The city, under the right thumb of Mayor Richard Daly, was in the throes of political upheaval. Chicago was the site of the 1968 Democratic National Convention, with its angry marches and police riots. The atmosphere was tense. In searching for an apartment, we had dozens of doors slammed in our faces by landlords angry with us for the mere fact that we were students, young people, the enemy. Then we met Jacob Zilberstein, an

Part 1

old bearded Jewish landlord in his seventies, who seemed above and beyond the political fray and who possibly recognized my surname from somewhere in his distant past. He rented us scruffy-looking students an apartment in the north end on busy Rogers Avenue near Loyola without question.

"I don't care if you show dirty movies," he said in his Yiddish accent, with a shrug of the shoulders, "just draw the drapes so the neighbours don't see."

But Europe had changed us forever. I no longer felt at home in the United States. Many of the strongest memories of my childhood were formed in Canada on vacations with my family, visiting my mother's Canadian relatives in Toronto and at cottages on Georgian Bay several hours north of the city. The Canadian lake country attracted me deeply and drew me to it. When I eventually came to live in Canada, I truly felt as if I were coming home.

II

Blackfly Season

THAT FIRST SUMMER AT the Farm was difficult and exquisite. I realized I had been hungering to spend an extended period in the countryside for my entire life. I wanted to simply sit by a stream and watch it go by — to experience that sense of profound peace and calm that I felt could be found in nature. But first, before I could relax and begin to appreciate my new environment, there was blackfly season to get through.

When I first saw the land, before buying it, it was high summer. Blackfly season was well over. But when we moved there the next spring, it was mid-May and the bug season was about to begin. The six of us — Wally, Wilf and Isobel, Steve and Shirley, and I — had a dream of being real farmers, a delusion that lasted exactly half a farming season. We had Big Plans. We drew endless maps of the field in front of the cabin, deciding where we would plant peas, radishes, lettuce, corn, beans, potatoes, squash, and tomatoes. We carefully selected packets of seeds from a mail-order catalogue. We bought tools: shovels, cultivators, rakes. We rented a Rototiller and began digging up the field, which turned out to be as much rock as soil. We cultivated, raked, and piled rocks and more rocks on the rocks that were already there. And as we worked and sweated, the blackflies came out.

The blackfly, in its larval stage, lives at the bottom of streams in cool, unpolluted water and feeds there on tiny organisms. Class *Insecta* is the largest class in the animal kingdom — the estimated three million species of insects outnumber all other plant and animal groups combined.

A blackfly is about a third the size of a mosquito (also a fly). In a close-up photo, the appearance of the blackfly with its bulbous abdomen bears a striking resemblance to my 1947 Chevy, a rather blunt instrument I bought for $200 from an old lady in the village of Wakefield near the Farm in the early 1970s. They tend to cluster in clouds about the victim's head (blackflies, not '47 Chevies), getting into the eyes, ears, nose, and mouth. In the old days, workers on survey crews or woodcutters in the bush slathered every bit of exposed skin in bacon fat and balsam gum to keep the bugs away. I doubt it worked. In fact, the bacon fat probably drew the interest of bears. They make no discernible sound and only hurt slightly when they bite (blackflies, not bears). Like tiny flying Draculas, they especially like to bite the neck or behind the ear.

That first spring, working with a cloud of pestering bugs about our heads, wasn't fulfilling our romantic view of farming and life in the country. Thus it was that these six proto-farmers could be seen, day after day, working the field on hot afternoons in long-sleeved shirts and straw hats, beekeeper's nets over our heads and faces. It wasn't pleasant, but it worked. (Several years later some of us resorted to working in the gardens at night using car headlights trained on the field, because blackflies only come out in daylight.)

Blackfly season usually started about the middle of May and ran until almost the middle of June — three to four weeks. At the same time, depending on moisture and temperature, mosquito season, which overlapped the end of blackfly season, would begin. If the weather had been hot and moist through the spring, the mosquitoes could be in full flower by the end of May, or later if April and May had been cool and dry. Mosquito season peaked for about three to four weeks, but mosquitoes could be a problem in certain summers until late August. Usually, however, the summer solstice marked the beginning of a period when one could spend an evening out of doors without being tortured mercilessly.

At the height of mosquito season, life could be exceedingly unpleasant. In an old cabin with ill-fitted windows and doors, mornings, evenings, and sometimes long, sleepless, humid nights were spent listening to the whine of thousands of mosquitoes at the screens, as well as the approach of interlopers who had found their way in. One learned to slap oneself in the forehead while dreaming. Many a morning I awoke to find blood-spattered tattoos on my pillow.

It was no wonder the members of our little community weren't getting along. Tight lodgings, lack of money, the hot, humid weather, and the bugs combined to dispel our illusions. That, plus the endless difficulties that arise when people try to live together, put an impossible stress on relationships. Wilf and Isobel, the "straightest" of the crew, took their red setter and disappeared down the road in their van never to be heard from again, while Wally saw the corn reach his knees and high-tailed it back to the United States, fed up and disillusioned.

Steve, Shirley, and I stuck it out for the rest of the summer when the bugs died down and life took on a lovely pace and cadence. In the full richness of that season, we got to know one another.

12

Steve and Shirley

SHIRLEY WAS THE ONLY one of our group with any real farming experience, having grown up on a farm near Nipigon, Ontario. She was also the only one who had spent a childhood without electricity.

Most of the rest of us were typical North American suburban kids. (There would later be two Germans, a handful of Québécois, and an Englishwoman, as well.) Shirley had pale skin with a Scandinavian winter-sun glow, long straight blond hair, sleepy blue eyes, and an infectious laugh. There was a bit of the pioneer woman about her — she never complained about the rough life, the weather, or our simple fare. She loved to party and, with her generosity and sparkling energy, made everyone feel good in her presence.

Steve was the moon to Shirley's sun. Like Shirley, he was an artist, a painter who was seduced by the beauty of wood and became an expert in marquetry. With his dark eyes and long brown hair, Steve bore a striking resemblance to Neil Young. A true artist with a lifelong commitment to his work, he had a brooding mystical bent and an insatiable curiosity for the natural world. Any iridescent or red-tattooed beetle, or any other insect that happened to land on his arm, was worth a long, penetrating study. Steve was curious about the constellations, the trees, the birds, everything.

He loved to play his flute by the side of a quiet lake and listen to the pure sounds echo across the water and through the surrounding forest. At the time he didn't seem to need much more than that, although his cache of instruments was eventually augmented with a saxophone, which brought a completely different aural atmosphere (more bear-like than bird-like) to the quiet of the forest.

The three of us spent hours sitting around the fire, cooking breakfast, lunch, and dinner outside when the weather was decent, and talking, talking, talking — about art, religion, philosophy, music, culture, books, the magic of numbers, wildlife, birds, wood, language, poetry, whatever came up. I was keenly interested in the etymologies, or roots, of words and always kept my copy of *Origins* by Eric Partridge close by and would look up words obsessively to the minor annoyance of the others. We seldom discussed politics, though — we had abjured politics simply by coming to this place in the country. We gave little or no thought to the current newspaper headlines and often didn't see a newspaper from one month to the next. We were fulfilling, with haughty nonchalance, the third part of Timothy Leary's admonition ("Tune in, turn on, drop out") — we had indeed "dropped out," rejecting a major part of the world's business. In our youthful and dreamy innocence, we believed we had other paths to explore.

Long evenings were spent cooking and eating and feeding the fire in the yard next to the cabin. We would watch the campfire's smoke drift out like a banner, unfolding across our valley as the dusk brought cool, heavy air to hold the smoke down. Someone might go inside to grab a flannel coat or a sweater as the dark came on. Once the sky was black, bats began to swing and dive around the cabin. It seemed a good sign. I preferred the Chinese view that bats are emblems of happiness and long life, to the Western view that bats are infernal creatures just waiting to get tangled in your hair and infect you with rabies.

Quite often that summer we talked long into the night by the outside firepit under a sky full of stars that seemed to hang lower and closer to the earth here than elsewhere. Sparks from the fire would fly up into the black in a vain attempt to become stars themselves. They always went out before they reached that high. The sparks, too, in their way, were innocents.

It was too dark to do dishes in the cabin at night. As washing dishes in a plastic basin by coal-oil lamp and candlelight is a slow and burdensome process, we often left the dishes lying in the grass about the outdoor fireplace with plans to do them the following morning. Late at night we could hear the raccoons licking them clean. In the morning we gathered them up, hauled a couple buckets of water from the spring, and attended to the main morning chore of washing dishes from the previous night and getting breakfast.

We soon found that living with no electricity and no running water involved a lot of hard work. In order to get water from the spring, we took a path that led from the front of the cabin down along the edge of the field to a place where previous occupants had installed a spring box about thirty yards from the house. The spring box, with a hinged lid, was made of cedar boards and had been set over the place where the spring gushed from the earth. I would open the lid and dip my two plastic buckets into the clear, ice-cold water. The buckets were deep and made of heavy white plastic that had once contained cherry and apple pie filling, obtained from a bakery in the village of Wakefield about twelve miles away.

Occasionally, we found live frogs in the spring box, but no one ever experienced stomach upset from the water. I once had it tested by the government health department — it contained a touch of bacteria but was considered safe for drinking. The water never stagnated because the boards that formed the box weren't tight, allowing the free flow of water through the cracks. This was either natural smarts or dumb luck on the part of the previous generations of tenants. A lot of things around the Farm were like that. Years after I left, when a friend who lived there decided to "improve" the spring by installing a concrete pipe with a three-foot diameter as a reservoir to collect water, it didn't work. Small animals would fall in and not be able to get out. The water stagnated during dry season, and the spring became unusable.

After a summer of delicious abandon — reading, writing, gardening, dissolving into the long days and evenings in the company of the natural world and good friends — after coming to love the sound of the whippoorwill calling its own name from the deep forest, the sound of the brook running and bubbling, the great quiet under the full moon of August, the year began to fold back like the curling petal of a fading flower. The nights grew cooler. That first summer was coming to an end.

The trees, the ferns in the forest and their precise shadows on the dirt road, the circling hawks — somehow this natural world entered me even as I entered it and I had come to love a place on the earth.

But summer truly was ending. Shirley and Steve headed into Wakefield to work through the winter. While there they bought a quantity of canvas and began to cut and prepare it for a teepee to bring back to the Farm the next spring. I stayed on alone, melting into the landscape, spending my days cutting wood by hand with a bucksaw, dead dry elms and diseased or dead black ash I had felled in the swamp and hauled out in long pieces on my shoulder. I became extremely familiar with sawtooth and axe, with the smell of pine and cedar, straight ash grain, the gnarled tough elm.

Suddenly, it was autumn and the pressure of winter's arrival was in the air. I was high on nature, effortlessly getting up each morning to watch the sunrise, delighted to be alive. Each morning after breakfast I swung my spade onto my shoulder and walked to the far end of the Farm where I was spending my days digging a new garden in a field I thought looked fertile. The sod was thick, the earth clotted deep with the roots of field grass. It was hard work, cutting a square of sod, lifting the block of soil, shaking the earth loose and tossing aside the remaining chunk of grass and soil that wouldn't let go.

I loved the work, the sweat, the feel of my body's muscles straining under the sun. I was alone. The loneliness was welcome — like a poet-hermit of ancient China, I had the sun and the moon as companions. Everything came alive then: clouds, the wind, animals, birds, trees. I would walk down the road, and the same stand of five or six quaking aspens always seemed to attract the wind to their leaves as I approached as if they were attempting to communicate with me in their own way.

Spending so much time alone was deeply calming. Once, after I had spent a full week without seeing another soul, my friend Wally came to visit. It was the oddest feeling — he seemed ghost-like, not solid, insubstantial. I almost felt as if I could see right through him. After a short while, things returned to normal, but I began to understand what Shakespeare meant when he wrote in *Hamlet*, "There are more things in heaven and earth, Horatio, than are dreamt of in your philosophy."

Before the summer had ended, when Steve and Shirley were still at the Farm, the farmer Louis and I agreed that he could cut and gather the hay in the field in front of my cabin. One afternoon late in August he showed up driving two massive workhorses that pulled a hay cutter, ready to work. His small family followed behind.

The field in front of the cabin was shaped like an open book. The spine of the book was the stream that cut across the centre of the field, its bed dry in every season except spring. Like the two sides of a book laid open, the two halves of the field rose steeply at first from the stream bed, then levelled out as they climbed to the field's edges.

The family set to work without delay, no one needing instructions, everyone knowing their jobs. Maria, his short, round wife, and the two kids, a girl about ten and a boy about twelve, walked in front of the horses and cutter, picking up rocks from the field and flinging them out of the way. With sharp, terse commands, Louis drove the workhorses. And what horses! The grey-white, seemingly identical Percherons were as light-footed as clouds, muscles rippling, hooves as big as dinner plates with hair hanging over them like long moss on rocks in a stream. They moved effortlessly, with no wasted motion, no tossing of the head and flitting about as one would see from faster, edgier horses. And when they were still, they were majestic.

While Louis worked, he was serious and unsmiling, focused on the job before him, the reins resting lightly in his hand. He seemed like an archaic, archetypal, larger-than-life Greek god in his chariot.

The family tossing stones, commands from Louis punctuating the silent afternoon of late summer, the *tish, tish, tish* of the cutter, the huge graceful horses — it all seemed like a scene from a medieval Book of Days depicting the month of August. Steve, Shirley, and I sat on the ground next to the cabin at the edge of the field watching the family work. We weren't merely looking into the fields of an illuminated manuscript but were gazing back in time at a living past. At the end, before heading back along the road to his own house, Louis turned to us with the slightest nod of the head, still unsmiling but acknowledging and thanking us in his subtle way. The wife and kids could barely look at us, taking only the occasional surreptitious glance.

After a week of fine, dry weather, Louis returned with a hay wagon pulled again by the two grand horses. The kids raked the hay into piles, which Louis scooped up with his pitchfork as the horses, heads held high, pulled the wagon forward and halted at his command. It seemed, at times, with those huge hands and that broad back, that Louis could effortlessly pitch piles of hay the size of a family sedan onto his wagon.

One evening in early September, after everyone else returned to the city, I was sitting alone in the cabin, reading after dinner by the light of a coal-oil lamp (I was *always* reading after dinner — there was literally nothing else to do and, luckily, nothing else I wanted to do). Dark was falling and a knock came at the door, surprising me, as this was an unusual occurrence. Normally, I could hear a car approaching along the dirt road or people talking in the silent field as they walked the path and neared the cabin. I opened the door on the rising cool of an autumn dusk, and recognized Louis's young son. He had a large paper bag in his hands, which he shoved in my direction without saying a word, his eyes wide with panic and painful shyness. Before I could say anything, he spun about, picked up his bicycle from the ground, and sped back along the path across the field.

Still standing in the doorway, an autumn sunset ripening in the sky to the west, I looked in the bag. It contained a dozen fat red tomatoes the size of grapefruits.

13
Soil and Stars

At the Farm I had the luxury of boundless time spent within a restricted space. I could put roots down deep and feel into the heart of the place, my fingers running through its soil. Even now the memories are etched somewhere in the old furrows of my brain — the view from the cabin as I stood in the open doorway on a summer evening: a steep hill close on the left where a thrush knocked like wood dripping; the line of hills on the right, farther away but higher, over which the sun descended; the field before me where, earlier, in mid-afternoon, monarch butterflies like blown leaves had wafted among the milkweed pods and where the stream cut through on a diagonal; and the sky running almost out to the horizon where the first star appeared like a promise of comfort.

And I realize with what unstated intimacy Louis would have come to know his circumscribed square of earth. I imagine he knew every pine and alder in the hills and fields, the contours of the land, and the moment a groundhog or mole skittered across his farm. He likely knew where the next wind was coming from and where it would disappear to and sensed from its taste how long winter would last and on which morning he would awake to find winter's back broken by the spring sun — he had been on the land for that long. A lifetime. He would notice a new frost crack in a rock on the cliff, smell the deer slipping into the silent enclosing bush at field's edge, would know by the end of June if the tomatoes this summer would ripen. I doubt he knew the names of the stars — Alnitak, Alnilan, Mintaka — but they appeared precisely in the night sky where he had expected, almost as if he had willed their appearance or that, somehow, his ability to imagine those shattered pearls into place and their appearance there were not separate events.

We were two men from the same century but different ends of it. Separate but linked. This natural world was what we had in common. For Louis, unable to read, it must have been different. When I looked at the staghorn sumac turning the field's edge into a frieze of antlers, I saw the words *staghorn* and *sumac* written in my head. He could not. Perhaps his world was more aural than mine, as words offered a richer panoply of sounds for him. I don't know. I can't imagine the world without written words. People have been writing for more than 5,000 years. My imagination lacks the ability to see back before then. But as we sank into the world, it sank into us, and Louis and I could not help but share these hills and fields, the sky and stars, the aurora of birdsong as it blossomed from obsidian night.

Part 2

I
Borisov on the Berezina

THE GATINEAU HILLS ARE covered in prototypical forest in the Laurentian mode offering a wide variety of trees: pine, spruce, trembling aspen, cedar, white birch, maple (including silver maple whose leaves flash from silver to white on a windy day), oak, elm, ironwood (also known as hop hornbeam), and many others.

Trees have a long and intimate connection to language, which can be discerned in the origins of many of the names we have for trees. Consider the beech tree, whose leaves early settlers found more comfortable than straw for stuffing mattresses. The word *beech* is cognate with *book*, likely from the ancient tradition of carving runes on soft beechwood sticks.

The countryside around Borisov and Minsk region, where my grandfather Simon was from in central Belarus, is similar to the countryside in the Gatineaus — less hilly but covered in forest of a similar type of mixed hardwood and softwood.

Today forest still covers 45 to 50 percent of the Borisov district. Hunting is a prime tourist attraction. In rural areas, hunters' houses for rent by the week are common ("There is a daily charge of $80 per guest to be paid for accommodation, boarding, sauna, and hunting" reads one of many Internet ads.) The town of Borisov lies on the main road from Warsaw to Moscow on the banks of the Berezina River. Borisov on the Berezina was a site that Napoleon and his doomed armies came to know well.

The Berezina River has been described as a "long grey ribbon," but we don't know if it was as grey as Napoleon's greys, Emir and Moscow, or what horse he was on when he crossed the river in late November 1812, sixty-six years before Simon's birth. Perhaps he was on another of his horses, Tauris, for example, or Roitelet, a chestnut. He had 150 horses in his lifetime.

Napoleon's retreat from Russia, when the Grande Armeé dissolved in the wintry fields and forests of Belarus, has been a prime symbol for failed military excursions ever since, and the chaotic French retreat around my grandfather's town of Borisov has its eerie echo in the Vietnam War. Napoleon's armies lost half a million men and 150,000 horses in several months in Belarus, after conquering and abandoning Moscow, which the Russians themselves had earlier torched to ensure that the French would be left with nothing more than a smoking ruin.

The disaster of Napoleon's retreat is well recorded (Tolstoy's *War and Peace* includes an important scene at the Berezina). On the return march, during the flight out of Russia in the autumn of 1812, the soldiers of the Grande Armeé, in summer uniforms, were so loaded down with booty from Moscow that they could barely walk. One account tells of a sergeant who was freighted, on his person and in his knapsack, with the following: his uniform (which he had to carry because he was dressed in a yellow waistcoat of padded silk and a cape lined with ermine), a half-bottle of liqueur, a woman's Chinese silk dress and riding cloak, several pounds of sugar, gold and silver ornaments, lockets, two silver-mounted pictures, a spittoon, a crucifix, a Chinese porcelain vase, and a piece of the cross of Ivan the Great, as well as his powder flask, firearms, and cartridge case.

Throughout November the French armies and three Russian armies were converging on Borisov. Napoleon knew he must cross the Berezina River before the Russians arrived in force or all was lost. The French were harassed constantly as they approached Borisov, and stragglers were hacked to pieces by Cossack horsemen. Meanwhile the Russians torched the bridge at Borisov before the French arrived. The French, however, managed to locate an area nearby where the river was sufficiently shallow, and sappers began quickly to build two bridges at this site.

As horses, men, and baggage began crossing the two makeshift bridges, the scene was one of utter chaos. A huge crowd of soldiers and vehicles funnelled into the narrow entrance to the bridges where many were trampled. They came under attack from well-placed Russian cannons on nearby hills. An already disorderly retreat turned into a rout. Those with horses and carts, wanting to save their booty, didn't hesitate

Part 2

to ride over those who had been injured, swinging swords to cut their way through women, children, and fellow soldiers.

Many drowned while trying to swim across the ice-filled river. Finally, one bridge collapsed carrying everyone on it into the Berezina, and the huge desperate crowd surged over to the only remaining bridge, crushing others in front of them or knocking them into the water.

As soon as the Duke of Bellune and his French troops fled across the bridge, they set it afire. The many wounded abandoned on the bridge slipped burning into the icy waters.

Descriptions of the crossing of the Berezina and the collapse of Napoleon's army sound eerily similar to the panicked retreat from Vietnam, the chaotic final hours of the U.S. presence there. The communist armies of Vietnam were quickly overwhelming the South Vietnamese army and the remaining U.S. forces. Any Americans still there, and many of their Vietnamese supporters, were desperate to get out.

In the last hours, hundreds of panicked people converged on the U.S. embassy in Saigon where American helicopters attempted to take them from the roof of the embassy to safety. People tried to scramble onto the choppers or hold on to them as they lifted off. Meanwhile, at the Saigon airport, airplanes took off before the back hatches were closed, children and adults falling out to their deaths.

The tumultuous, chaotic exit from Saigon is one of the most memorable images of the Vietnam War, a war replete with images. These scenes of desperation from Saigon are burned into the collective memory of anyone old enough to have witnessed them on television at the time.

In 1878, sixty-six years after Napoleon's retreat, Simon Frutkin was born in that same town of Borisov. When Simon walked in the woods near his town, I wonder what birds he might have heard there, what animal tracks he might have seen in the snow, if perhaps he might have found a French coin in the earth as I once discovered an 1888 oversize Canadian penny in my garden in Quebec. (An Ottawa coin expert told me it was worth five cents.)

A thousand years ago a Chinese poet said the soil of the fields, long after the battles had finished, was more bones than soil. One can picture the farmers around Borisov planting potato seedlings in their fields, unaware the roots grew through the eye sockets and twined into the empty thoughtless skulls of long-dead French soldiers. But the earth itself cleanses everything — all past deeds, all memory of good and evil. When I worked in the garden at the Farm, I would often take up a handful of soil and smell it. I appreciated that aroma — slightly resinous, fresh, clean. I have no doubt that knowledgeable farmers can garner a wealth of information from the scent of a handful of soil. We are fortunate, however, that we cannot clearly read the entirety of the past in it.

Simon traversed the fields and forests west of Borisov in his flight to America. "Don't go when the snow is falling," an older, wiser friend would have said. "You will be too easy to track. Nor should you go when the earth is soft and the mud can reveal your trail. Go when the earth has dried. In late summer or early autumn. Beware the hunters. Beware the bears. Do not try to swim the rivers for they are fast and deep. But, above all, do not go in winter. Remember Napoleon."

2

Winter

Winter was, indeed, a time for staying close to home. At the Farm I slept in one of the tiny bedrooms (it had three) on the second floor of the cabin, a long way from the fire in the wood stove. By morning a glass of water next to my bed was often frozen solid. My mother had given me an ancient eiderdown blanket passed down from her Canadian mother, so I was never cold in bed. I slept with my head under the covers all night, working up a fine fug (as the Irish say), and it worked a charm. But getting out of bed in the morning was difficult. Abandoning the warmth for the ice-cold shock of day was an action to be resisted as long as possible.

Part 2

Once the decision had finally been made, I would leap up, throw on frigid clothes, jeans, flannel shirt, sweater, jacket, rush into the backyard with a hatchet, chop kindling, hurry back into the cabin. Occasionally, the firebox in the wood stove, which I had stoked with huge logs the night before on retiring, still retained a few coals. I'd throw in the kindling and newspaper and get the fire started again in earnest.

The first hour of any winter morning involved standing next to the wood stove waiting for it to heat up and begin warming the cabin. I'd boil water and make cowboy coffee, throwing the grounds directly into the pot of water, heating it and pouring it carefully into a cup, ensuring the grounds stayed at the bottom of the pot. A piece or two of homemade bread toasted right on the iron plates of the stove was breakfast. By midmorning I could remove my coat and sit in the comfort of the kitchen.

Winter was a time of wood: gathering wood, sawing it, chopping, hauling, and burning it. I carried armloads of elm and ash, sometimes maple, oak, or beech, from the woodshed outside the back door to the large wood box next to the stove, filling it with enough wood to last a day and night if the weather was cold, perhaps two days if it turned mild.

Through direct experience I learned a great deal of practical information about trees and firewood. Much of this knowledge appears obvious to a Canadian who has spent any time at all in the bush, but for a city dweller or suburbanite the forest and its contents remain something of a mystery. I learned that standing elm and ash, once they've died, have a tendency to lose their bark and dry quite nicely in the forest. White birch is never found in this state. The papery bark clings to the dead tree and the wood underneath rots quickly. Oak is too high up the mountains to get at easily. Maple is excellent, but there never seemed to be much dead maple near my cabin. Beech could only be found in small patches here and there or in larger stands higher on the hillsides. Aspen, pine, spruce, cedar — all the softwood trees burn dirty and fast. They're good for kindling but not for feeding a fire over a long winter's evening — you would have to throw logs into the wood stove every ten minutes. Because the cabin stood on the edge of a "dry" swamp, elm and ash were the trees most available. The property, especially in the low areas, was thick with dead, dry trees, their bark shed, their wood the colour of bone or grey-white sky.

I would head off into the swamp with my bucksaw, heavy winter boots with felt liners on my feet, a flannel jacket on my back. I'd hunt out a likely tree of deadwood, saw it down, and cut it up into four-foot sections that I could carry out on my shoulder (or shorter pieces if it was a thicker tree). If the tree was particularly large, I'd have to chop a *V* into the side in the direction I wanted it to fall. Then I'd saw away and hope it actually fell away from me. I never had one land on my head, although, often enough, the saw stuck (due to the tree's shifting weight) or the tree's branches got hung up in other nearby trees when it fell. Once the main trunk was down, I trimmed off any branches with the axe and sawed the trunk into lengths I could carry.

After the cutting came the hauling. I'd lift the log onto my shoulder and carry it out of the swamp and up to the cutting yard next to the cabin. Once there, I'd throw it on the ground and head back for the next piece. No matter how cold it was, this work always warmed me. Quite often I'd be down to my flannel shirt in twenty minutes. As the saying goes, "wood warms twice." If the snow was deep, the work was that much harder. Hauling four-foot sections of log on my shoulders, each step taking me up to my waist in snow — I could do it all day. I was young and fit and in no hurry.

Once I got the sections hauled to the yard, I'd set a log up across the sawhorse, get the saw started on the log, and then lean into it with long, steady strokes, two hands on the handle of the saw. If a bucksaw is sharp, it can cut through an eight-inch-thick log in ten or twelve strokes. I'd cut them into three pieces, each about sixteen inches long, for splitting. The thinner branches I cut up and left unsplit, ready for the fire. The winter cutting yard was my outdoor playground. Quite often the snow around the yard was up to my armpits or ears, but I kept an area clear around the sawhorse and the splitting block, which was the largest, toughest piece of log I could find (usually elm), about two feet high and set on end. The ground would be inches deep in oat-coloured sawdust from my work with the bucksaw.

Part 2

I'd pause, stand in my winter clearing, and breathe the crisp, glassy air. Eyes closed, staring at the strong winter sun, I'd let the rays warm me, turning the insides of my eyelids golden. The brilliant Canadian winters stood in stark contrast to the winters of my youth in Cleveland, the second least sunny city in the United States, after Seattle. The winters in Cleveland, on the south shore of Lake Erie, tended to the grey and sleety, and were nowhere near as long as winters in Quebec.

As soon as a pile of logs accumulated, I started splitting them. With straight-grained ash it was easy. The axe swung through in one smooth sweep, the log falling in perfect halves. I loved the smell of ash — couldn't resist its sweet resinous powdery perfume. Elm was another matter. The wood always had a rank smell, the grain twisted and gnarled. Better to burn it whole if possible. Nothing escapes fire. Even those elm fibres seemingly made of twisted steel wire melted like butter in the inferno of the wood stove. Elm burned long and hot and, with the prevalence of Dutch elm disease, there was plenty of dead elm at hand.

Once in a while I would haul out the sledgehammer and wedges to split larger, tougher logs. The sledgehammer was huge, must have weighed fifteen pounds, and the heavy steel wedges had sharp, broken flanges around the heads, dangerous to the touch. The used sledge and wedges were passed on to me by my father. At the end of its round straight wooden handle the ponderous lump of the sledge felt like an anvil. This Cro-Magnon approach to wood splitting lacked the lyrical qualities of the axe, with its handle curved and sensuous. Despite the sledge and wedges, a few large, tough elm pieces defeated me for years and never would be split. (These found their fiery fate in the outdoor pit late on summer nights.) After the sledge, the axe felt light and playful, a joy to swing, more bird than plow.

3
Bread

WINTER WAS ALSO THE season for baking. With the wood stove going full blast twenty-four hours a day from December through March, the oven was always on and always available. My particular specialty was bread.

Like most kids in the suburbs of the 1950s in North America, I was raised in a white-bread world. Looking back on those times, I believe white bread stood for all that was wrong with that world: soft (even the crust was soft), mushy, tasteless, over-processed, lacking anything genuine or true in its essential nature. It was already sliced so you were saved the bother of having to lift a knife. It never went mouldy. A wondrous product for modern times, absolutely perfect in every way — each slice the right size for the toaster, each loaf exactly the same number of slices, each crust the perfect shade of pale brown — no, not even brown but tan. Tan-coloured crust — the perfect way to suggest crust with none of the reality.

I recall as a youngster (I'm sure every child has done this) taking a piece of white bread and trying to see how small a ball I could squeeze it into. It came out about the size of a grape. How much flour was actually in each slice? Half a teaspoon?

At the Farm I made bread in the true, old-fashioned way. On one of their several visits, my parents, at my request, bought me an eighty-pound bag of wheat berries at a health food store. Wheat berries were the real thing — the stuff out of which flour was milled. The whollest of whole wheat. Nothing fancy here — no sourdough, no black Russian rye, no flax seed. I had a hand grinder, which I attached to the side of the wooden kitchen table. Into this I poured the wheat berries. I grasped the thin curved handle of dark polished wood and began to turn, left palm flat on the table to keep everything steady. It took me about forty minutes of hard work to grind enough flour for two loaves of bread. I didn't care — I had little money and plenty of time, all the time in the world. Like the drifting snow out my kitchen window, the flour collected in the bowl under the grinder. It was hard work, but as with woodcutting, it kept me warm.

I didn't often bother with yeast because I had read that if bread were kneaded properly and sufficiently, yeast came out naturally from the flour through this physical process. I didn't think seventeen big-boned Ukrainian farmwomen could have kneaded yeast out of that flour, but I was willing to try.

The chapter on bread in the classic *Joy of Cooking* begins with a wonderful lesson in political *in*correctness: "Once upon a time, when the English language was young, the word from which the modern English 'lady' sprang meant 'loaf-kneader,' and the verb 'to knead' has even prehistoric origins! To our own and our families' distinct profit — and with little effort — we housewives can become 'ladies' again." (The exclamation point appears in the original.) What do the Rombauers Irma and Marion mean "with little effort"? That was the 1950s salve: have it all without any effort.

I decided to look up *lady* to see if the *Joy* was having us on. I consulted my etymological dictionary and found that *lady* comes from the Old English *hlafdige*, or "loaf-kneader." *Lord*, *lady*, and *loaf* are all cognates. What this says about the importance of bread in our culture is highly suggestive, how bread is interwoven with family life, the owning of land (the *lord's* acreage), and so on.

But back to basics, the staff — and stuff — of life. I added the liquid. A bit of milk, if I had it; some water, a dollop of honey or a spoon of molasses, an egg, if I had it. A tat of butter, some salt. Then I rolled up my sleeves and dived in.

Once all the ingredients were thoroughly mixed, the push and pull of kneading started. There is something marvellous and essential about kneading bread. One becomes the original potter kneading a lump the size of a fetus, the dough like clay or mud. A living being swells under your working hands. Fold it over, push it away, fold it over again, push away again — a bit like rocking a cradle but with more physical involvement, more effort and energy. Knead it until it's "smooth, elastic and satiny" as the *Joy* says.

After the kneading, I covered the bowl with a cloth and placed it in the warming oven on the wood stove for an hour or so to rise. The warming oven is the area at the top of a wood stove, usually with a door, where one stores baking tins, pot lids and other kitchen oddments. An excellent location for letting dough rise. I left the warming oven door open if the fire was booming. Too warm and the dough rose too fast and collapsed (although there was little real chance of that, considering the heaviness of the flour used).

Then I went away and did something else, like carrying in armloads of firewood to the wood box or heading to the spring for water. A while later I returned to the warming oven, took out the bowl, punched down the risen dough, kneaded it some more, split it in half, and plopped each half into a greased metal baking tin. These I put back in the warming oven to rise. I didn't worry too much about the time — there was no clock on the wood stove and I didn't wear a watch. The sun was up there in the sky somewhere; if I really wanted to know, I could look out the window for the time.

After an appropriate while, I came back to the warming oven, took the two tins of dough, and placed them in the baking oven in the stove. Placement was important because everything depended on the state of the fire at that moment and the baker's ability to read the heat output of the wood stove. If the fire was raging and the tins were placed toward the firebox side of the oven, the bread would burn on that side. A steady fire with no peaks and troughs was best — the Middle Way in all things — perhaps a bed of maple coals that would last a long time and keep their heat. This wasn't the moment to load the firebox with dry cedar or spruce. The door of the oven had a temperature gauge, but it didn't mean much. Better to know your fire, know your stove, know your oven, know your bread. Trial and error.

About this time I started salivating as the aroma of baking bread permeated the cabin. When the bread was done, I removed the pans from the oven and plunked the two loaves onto a wooden cutting board. My bread was heavy, earthy, weighty, seldom more than one and a half to two inches high at its thickest point. This wasn't ersatz. It had something in common with the world of minerals. I'd take serrated knife in hand and cut a sizable piece from the end. The crust was a deep burnished brown, and shiny. I'd slather butter on the bread, which was still soft and steaming. Have you ever tasted something so good that you had to sit down after the first bite? Bread. Basic bread. A gift of the earth. The Joy of Cooking indeed!

Having an oven that's on continuously (as in a wood-fired cookstove that is also used for house heating) can have its disadvantages. Once, during a meal with friends, I placed a dozen dinner buns on a tray in the oven and promptly forgot them. I had no need to use the oven for several weeks, since spring had arrived and I was doing little baking at that time, although I fired up the stove every morning and evening to warm the cabin and to cook dinner.

When I finally opened the oven weeks later for some unrelated reason, I found the formerly white dinner buns were now pure charcoal, absolutely black through and through, and nearly weightless, but holding their original shape. They looked like little bombs an anarchist would throw.

4
Conscription Crisis

ON A SUMMER DAY in late June 1914 in Sarajevo, a nineteen-year-old anarchist and terrorist named Gavrilo Princip assassinated Archduke Franz Ferdinand and his wife. The First World War was the result. That war would also precipitate, ultimately, the first of two major conscription crises in Canada.

The fiercest resistance to a Canadian draft came from Quebec. During the First World War, a majority of Québécois saw little sense in going overseas to fight to defend Britain and the Crown.

Henri Bourassa, an influential Member of Parliament and founder of *Le Devoir*, Quebec's most prestigious newspaper, had opposed the use of Canadian troops in the Boer War in 1900. Along with Thomas D'Arcy McGee, one of the Fathers of Confederation, he strongly supported a

Canada that was officially neutral like Switzerland. When the Second World War started, Bourassa opposed conscription and published a book entitled *What Do We Owe England?* in which he argued vehemently against conscription and for official Canadian neutrality.

Bourassa, a Quebec nationalist, was intensely disliked in English Canada. An editorial in the Toronto newspaper, the *Globe*, stated in 1918: "This unworthy demagogue has devoted his energies and abilities to the development of a discontented, unhappy, suspicious sentiment among his compatriots. If there were grievances, he sought to magnify them. If there were wounds, he salted them."

There were indeed plenty of grievances for Bourassa to magnify and numerous wounds to salt. In 1912 Ontario had passed Regulation 17, a bill that severely limited French-language schooling for the French minority in the province. French Canadians viewed this as a direct attempt at assimilation. In addition, it was felt that French-speaking volunteers in the military were shoddily treated, and francophones were irked that the language of command was limited to English only.

By 1915 the number of volunteers signing up was declining rapidly. The government decided to allow any civilian organization to raise an infantry battalion. This resulted in the formation of two battalions of "bantams," men under five feet two inches in height, as well as a battalion of teetotalers. Among volunteers across the country, the vast majority were those who had actually been born in Britain and immigrated to Canada. Although only 10 percent of Canada's population was British-born, almost half of all Canadians who served in the war had been born in the British Isles.

The French of Quebec felt no similar attachment to the motherland of France, likely because French immigration to Canada had slowed to a trickle by the early twentieth century. Between 1900 and 1920 more than 1.3 million British immigrated to Canada. In the same period, only 28,000 immigrants came from France, slightly more than those who emigrated from Finland.

Across Canada, as the war progressed, fewer and fewer volunteers were to be found. Those in farming, whether in English or French Canada, were particularly reluctant to leave the land. Recruitment was so low that the 167th Battalion even tried raffling an automobile to attract recruits in Quebec City, with little success. French Canadians comprised roughly 30 percent of the Canadian population but a mere 4 percent of volunteers.

Opposition to the 1917 conscription bill was fierce among labour, farmers, and many non-British Canadians. Riots broke out in Montreal, and conscription was widely and publicly denounced throughout Quebec. Rioting crowds attacked the offices of pro-conscription newspapers, and the home of the owner of Montreal's *Daily Star* was dynamited. Troops brought in from Toronto to quell a riot in Quebec City opened fire on anti-conscription demonstrators, killing four.

Among English Canadians conscription appeared to be grudgingly supported, although of the 404,000 registrants across the country, 380,000 sought some form of legal exemption (94 percent nationwide; 98 percent in Quebec). Many draftees unable to gain legal exemption simply went into hiding. By the end of the First World War, there were 24,139 official "defaulters" across Canada. In Quebec specifically, an incredible 40.83 percent of those ordered to report evaded the draft. At official levels the two halves of the nation remained fundamentally and bitterly split on the issue.

In 1917 even the British Parliament was debating conscription. At the time an anti-conscriptionist British MP, Richard C. Lambert, declared, with all the oratorical flare and overuse of majuscules typical of the recent Victorian era: "Voluntary service lies at the root of Liberalism, just as Conscription is the true weapon of Tyranny."

At the outbreak of the Second World War the memories of the Great War were still fresh in people's minds and the previous conscription crisis hadn't been forgotten. When registration was implemented (Prime Minister William Lyon Mackenzie King never thought he would have to implement full conscription), the ebullient and corpulent mayor of Montreal, Camillien Houde, stated that he opposed national registration and called it "unequivocally a measure of conscription." The federal government censored his statements and threw him in jail where he stayed for four years without proper trial.

Exemption from registration was offered to a wide-ranging collection of people: clergymen, judges, RCMP, policemen, firemen, prison and mental asylum workers, Mennonites, and conscientious objectors. Later in the war the Sons of Freedom Doukhobors, most of whom lived in British Columbia, regularly ignored call-up notices and staged nude parades if any pressure was put on them.

In 1942 a countrywide plebiscite showed that 72.9 percent of Quebeckers opposed conscription. In a sudden reversal of position, Mackenzie King implemented full conscription in 1944 when it appeared the numbers in the armed forces would be insufficient. Pressure from the United States and Britain played a part. At one point American President Franklin Delano Roosevelt, in response to Québécois resistance to a draft, sent a letter to Mackenzie King proposing an unofficial assimilation project for all francophones of Quebec and New England.

At that time only 8 percent of French speakers in Canada supported conscription. Throughout the country those twenty-one to twenty-nine years of age were most opposed, while those over fifty-four gave the strongest support to conscription. Once again the country was split along linguistic lines (and age lines, too) when it came to a draft.

After conscription was declared, the RCMP and military police began to raid public places looking for "absentees." It was during one of these raids on a country hotel in northern Ontario that Louis Drouin and his brother, Albert, were picked up. Active resistance to a draft had become widespread. In Drummondville, Quebec, a hundred-man official raiding party looking for absentees was attacked by a mob. Vehicles were smashed and overturned and a pitched battle that lasted three hours took place in the streets. At the other end of the country as many as a thousand French-speaking and other soldiers training in British Columbia commandeered their camps and weapons and refused to be shipped overseas.

Throughout Quebec resistance was fierce. In the region of Chicoutimi near the village of St. Ambroise, there is a mountain called Montagne des Conscrits (there is a Refuge des Conscrits in the Alps, as well). During the Second World War, Montagne des Conscrits served as a hiding place and refuge for local young men seeking to avoid the draft. They had camps in the mountain forest and spent their time cutting wood and hauling it down to the edge of the village where others collected it. When the RCMP and the military police were in the area, the local women would hang Hudson's Bay blankets outdoors on their wash lines as a signal to the men on the mountain to avoid coming down and to go deeper into the forest to hide there or in caves.

5
Snow

WINTER TAKES UP A lot of space and time in this story because winter in Quebec feels (and sometimes actually is) three times longer than any other season.

To sit in the cabin and gaze out the window at the falling snow, the wood stove filling the cabin with its radiant warmth, was a simple pleasure. The air of the cabin was redolent with the smell of wood and a touch of smokiness. Perhaps the smell of coffee and baking bread would be mixed in. The water in the bucket was pure. The unsullied snow was everywhere for miles around, covering every hill and valley, hanging on the branches of the trees, banked around the cabin and filling the fields, and more was falling. There was nowhere to go, nothing that must be done. Winter would not be hurried; it took the time it needed.

One night I recall going to bed (I sometimes slept downstairs in the living room to be close to the stove during the coldest months) and the level of the snow was well below the windows. When I awoke the next morning, the snow had climbed to the top of the first panes — it had snowed almost three feet in one night.

I went out after breakfast. The world was transformed. It took me hours to shovel the area outside my door and the path to the outhouse. I spent the afternoon clearing snow from around my sawhorse and chopping block, the mounds surrounding me now well higher than my head.

For walking in the forest after a heavy snow, I preferred snowshoes to cross-country skis as the former allowed me to go almost anywhere in the woods, including over rocky areas or through thick bush where skis could become caught in the tangle. In the forest I caught occasional glimpses of rabbits or other wildlife, but the true attraction was the silence, the world muffled and wrapped.

After taking a hike up the hills, I returned to woodcutting. There was always woodcutting and splitting to be done. Once the cutting area had been cleared of snow, revealing the gold and brown of wood chips and sawdust at my feet, I set to work again. If the sun had come out, the light would be brilliant, the trees in the field casting sapphire-blue shadows as if the snow held the memory of water within it.

Winter had another face, as well. From mid-January to mid-February is called "the dead of winter" for good reason.

One year, in early February, the air was so frigid that trees in the cedar swamp out my back door sounded like rifle shots when they popped with the frost in the long dark evenings. One evening I walked the two and half miles into the village of Wolf Lake after dinner. As I owned no car at the time, I would hike to the village whenever I needed groceries and carry them home in a knapsack. This particular evening I was collecting a cheque from the municipality for work I had done in the late fall cutting brush with a bucksaw and axe along the road that passed through the Farm. The council had insisted that I attend the monthly municipal meeting in order to collect my $30. They wanted to ensure that someone, anyone, would show up at their meetings, which were tedious beyond belief, dealing as they did in the minutiae of local zoning, municipal plowing, and taxes.

As I walked down the road, the trail of the Milky Way echoing my path, the temperature began to plummet. I pulled down the face mask that was folded up inside my toque, making me look like a latter-day terrorist. But at least I wouldn't get frostbite on my nose. My lined canvas greatcoat had a hood and a heavy zipper as well as snaps down the front. I hardly ever found the need to snap it up, but that evening the icy air was penetrating. Tugging off my heavy leather mitt, I pushed the first metal snap at chest level. The skin of my thumb stuck to it. Luckily, it wasn't stuck for long and I was able to rip it off without leaving any skin behind. Jamming the mitt back on, I picked up the pace, never thinking of turning back. The $30 was my grocery money for the next few weeks.

The road into the village skirted Wolf Lake, which was iced over and snow-covered, and passed a number of small village houses. Not a soul was outdoors. Arriving at the Foran general store, I entered, whipping my toque and mask off my head. Thomas, the thin, red-faced Anglo proprietor, greeted me.

"Evening." He nodded.

We chatted for a few moments. Then he stopped suddenly and looked at me. "Holy smokes! Did you walk here? It's minus thirty-five tonight!" (Fahrenheit in those days.)

I nodded. "Have to go to the municipal meeting. Pick up my pay."

He shook his head, not sure whether I was a genuine nutter or just plain stupid.

I left for the meeting, making my way farther down the empty village street to the little municipal building. Taking a seat on a metal folding chair, I waited with four other local people while the three councillors present discussed municipal business. They made me wait until the end of the meeting to collect my pay. I'm sure they wanted to guarantee they didn't lose their already skimpy audience. And what a meeting it was. It might have been earth-shattering, momentous decisions being made at the front table where the three councillors (all men) sat facing us, but I wouldn't know because the entire meeting was held in French — a particularly gnarly local French at that, resembling Algonquin as much as the French of France — and my language skills were just not up to the task. So I sat and waited patiently for almost two hours, my feet sitting in the puddle left by the snow that melted off my boots. I removed my toque and mitts. Pulled off my scarf. Opened my coat. Wished I could take my sweater off. The room wasn't merely warm — it was hot and uncomfortable. Somehow it seemed appropriate that a little plastic palm tree sat in a corner of the room. Occasionally, I would pick up a few comments by one of the councillors or a member of the audience (also all men). One of them drove the municipal snowplow, and endless discussions ensued about arcane details of road widths, complaints, and scheduling. But then I would lose the thread of the discussion and never learn how things were resolved. It was all very frustrating and tedious. I went to numerous municipal meetings over the years, and they were all like that: a little overheated room in hell.

After the meeting, I walked back at double pace, as the temperature was dropping further. No time to look at the stars.

The next night brought the lowest temperature I ever recorded during my stay at the Farm. A frightening minus fifty-five Fahrenheit. I stayed close to the stove.

I was beginning to realize what the old-timers meant by "cabin fever." Days went by without the temperature moderating. I cut wood, fed the stove (which proved voracious in this frigid weather), and read. No one came to visit. The city felt a million miles away. It was the genuine hibernation that is winter in the bush. If you could enjoy it, it proved marvellously peaceful, but if you started fighting against the boredom, who knew where that great white void could lead you.

One night I was feverishly wondering what the hell I was doing there: no woman, no money, no friends, bored out of my skull. I was depressed and angry. Suddenly, a wave of rage washed up through me, and before I knew it I had picked up a wooden kitchen chair and was smashing it down on the wood stove. The chair shattered but, luckily, the iron stove was untouched, of course, as it was so heavy it took six strong men to lift it. Luckily, the fever passed and I did no further harm to any other furniture that night.

Eventually, bit by bit, winter began to lose its icy grip. Drops of melting snow fell from the roof in sparkling lines, like music in the sunlight, as the books I finished piled up around me. Messy spring was on its way.

Part 2

6
Maple Sap

During the winter, it was impossible not to dream about spring. One sunny winter afternoon I began to plan how I would tap a nearby stand of maple trees to begin making maple syrup as soon as the thaw began to set in. In preparation for this, I cut staghorn sumac branches to carve into maple taps.

The field in front of the cabin was stitched with sumac along its edge where it met the forest. I had picked the large red cone-like sumac flowers the previous summer and made a brew from them that tasted like rosehip tea, only better, less acidic. I had read in the *Whole Earth Catalog* about using sumac branches for taps, and I realized I could save the cost of buying metal ones and be ecological at the same time. It was the old way, and I was enamoured of the old ways because they used what was in the environment. For me it was a statement about self-sufficiency. In addition, I was curious to see if it would actually work.

Staghorn sumac is used for this purpose because many of the branches are about the right size, approximately as big around as one's thumb. You begin by cutting the branches into two-inch sections. The core of the branches is filled with soft pulp, which can be easily removed from these short sections with coat-hanger wire, leaving the outer, harder wood. Then one end can be cut at an angle to provide a drip spout, while the other end is whittled down slightly for easy driving into the holes drilled in the trees.

The maple sap begins to run when the sun is sufficiently strong in the daytime to begin to melt the snow, usually sometime in March. It starts first on hillsides with a southern exposure. Once I felt that the weather was right, I made my way to an area on the Farm where I had previously come across a stand of old maples, northeast of my cabin, across the dirt road, and beyond a long field. These were the largest maple trees on the property, each about two to three feet across. Over an area of several acres stood approximately thirty trees. Slogging through the softening, waist-high snow, I pulled a pile of gear on a sled: my hand-operated augur for drilling the holes, a bag of the homemade sumac taps, a tower of nested plastic buckets with handles, hammer and nails, and a square galvanized tub for boiling sap.

Arriving in the maple grove, I gauged the positioning of the trees and placed the tub approximately in the middle. I started by setting the taps. Using the hand augur, I drilled a hole at a slight upward angle in the tree at mid-chest level, then lightly hammered in a sumac tap, pounded in a nail above the tap and hung a bucket on it. It was slow going as the area was still at least a yard deep with wet snow. By the time the maples finished running three weeks later, the snow would be gone completely, except for the odd white patch in shady areas, and the first watery green shoots would be visible on the forest floor. Around the grove I trudged, hammering in the homemade taps, hanging plastic buckets, and listening to the *plink, plink, plink* of the maple sap beginning to drip.

I went back to my cabin to fetch a fifty-gallon metal drum that I pulled back to the grove on the sled as before. I put my axe and saw inside the drum, since I needed to cut plenty of firewood to keep the fire roaring to cook down the sap. Once back in the grove, I collected dry kindling from low-hanging dead branches and set a fire inside the metal barrel. When the fire was blazing, I poured a few buckets of sap I had collected into the tub and placed it over the opening of the barrel. It was sheer luck that the tub fitted perfectly inside the barrel's mouth and yet didn't go all the way in because the tub was slightly wider at the top than the bottom and rounded at the corners. Because I was placing a square tub inside a round barrel, spaces were left for air to go in and smoke to come out at the four sides. Experience had taught me that this was a much more efficient boiler than an open-air fire, which dissipated a high percentage of the heat required. And, in fact, a tremendous amount of heat was needed to boil down thirty to forty gallons of thin, watery sap into one gallon of thickened syrup. Luckily, the forest all around was filled with deadwood, both on the ground and standing, so I had no trouble keeping the hungry fire fed.

For the next three weeks my days consisted of starting a fire in the barrel when I arrived in the bush in the morning, emptying the buckets of watery sap into the tub (making sure to remove any detritus that had fallen: bits of bark, moths, a mouse once, et cetera), gathering firewood, perhaps making myself a cup of cowboy coffee using maple sap instead of water, and watching winter leave and spring arrive in the maple bush. One day for lunch I boiled a bunch of white tapering parsnips in sap water. The root vegetables had remained all winter under the snow and earth in my garden and were still edible and fresh when I pulled them in the spring. Once cooked in the sap, the parsnips gained a delicious extra measure of sweetness.

As the days wore on, the snow gradually melted away. The sun grew strong and I would be down to my flannel shirt sleeves by afternoon. Once the sap had sweetened and thickened into syrup — it took thirty to forty gallons of sap to make one gallon of syrup — I ladled it into glass Mason jars, which I took home with me at the end of the day. I had put two or three taps in each of the largest trees and eventually made about thirty gallons of syrup, approximately one gallon per maple tree, most of which I sold to friends and acquaintances at a reasonable rate. I don't know how few cents I made per hour; it was probably pennies. Somehow it didn't matter.

7
Poverty and Wealth

IN THE EARLY 1970S, I once lived an entire year on $600. I don't know how I did it, but back then anything seemed possible. I had few bills. No mortgage, no utilities, no gas and no insurance (because I had no car), and no meat to buy because I was a vegetarian at the time. No frivolous entertainment expenses because I had nowhere to go and, having no car, couldn't get there, anyway. I always bought books, though — used books and cheap paperbacks. I wasn't looking for beautiful objects or costly collectors' items but ideas, stories, the wealth of other imaginations to spark my own.

I ate, for the most part, from my own garden, and bought a bit of coal oil to light my evenings. My share of the annual taxes on the Farm at the time were a pittance, under $50, and I hadn't yet discovered fine French wines. I made my own bread and other baked goods, although I had to buy milk, cheese, pasta, beer, and a few other groceries.

With a little help from generous family and friends, I was able to get by. My parents sent money on every occasion and hauled up box loads of canned goods and dry goods when they visited. My mother was the very essence of a movable feast, taking the contents of entire grocery shelves everywhere she went.

I was able to earn the little money I needed by working a few short-term jobs. I cut brush along my own road for the municipality, built a few decks with friends, did a bit of demolition work, was the night janitor at the Wakefield Hotel for several months one winter when I lived in Wakefield. I also did some craft work (I became an expert in the little-known world of wooden chimes) and attended a few craft fairs in Ottawa over the years (where I once sold thirty copies of my first book of self-published poetry). For a couple of winters, usually for about four to six weeks, I moved into Ottawa and lived with friends Paul and Colleen. One winter in the city I earned a reputation as the worst waiter ever to jumble an order at Nate's Deli on O'Connor Street. Another winter I worked shovelling snow and spraying water at night on the world's longest frozen canal, the Rideau. Nothing compares with standing alone at 4:00 a.m. holding a hose, spraying a fine mist into the minus forty degree darkness.

One lonely winter day I remember a fellow draft resister, John B., who worked at Ritchie's Feed and Seed in Ottawa, arriving with a thirty-pound bag of dried yellow-eyed beans — an unexpected and most welcome gift. I became a world expert at bean stew. Thirty pounds of beans can go a long way, even when one sups on bean stew four times a week. My life had a richness and simplicity exemplified by those bean stews. I'd soak and cook the yellow-eyed beans and throw in whatever I had (stews are forgiving that way): onions, garlic, carrots, chard, spinach, tomatoes, beet greens, potatoes, broccoli, beets, red and/or green cabbage, green beans, zucchini, peas, parsnips, and sometimes wild plants such as lamb's quarters; as well as handfuls of fresh or dried herbs: summer savory, basil, thyme, oregano, sage, whatever was available and abundant. Salt and pepper to taste. With homemade bread, they were some of my most memorable meals.

Once my friend and neighbour, Dave, came over and gave me a bottle of dandelion wine he'd made. I promptly put it in a lower cupboard and forgot about it. The next winter he came to visit and asked if I had ever drunk it. We dug it out and drank it then. It proved to be nectar, a bit of summer light in the depths of winter's darkness.

Another time Colleen gave me a huge stack of back issues of the *New York Times Magazine*. What a delight. Here I was in the middle of nowhere (actually, the edge of nowhere, not even the middle) and the heart and mind of the intellectual world was being offered to me page after page. And, most important, I had the one ingredient absolutely essential to engaging with this stack of great writing and thought: I had time.

Meanwhile, Paul, while attending a carpenter's training school in Guelph, Ontario, took as one of his projects the construction of wooden-framed screens for every window in my cabin to replace the ill-fitted screening I had simply stapled into the window openings. He and Colleen showed up with them the next spring, and they were duly installed.

8

Teepee

THE SECOND SPRING AT the Farm began with the arrival of Steve and Shirley with their teepee, and Paul and Colleen with a tent. The latter set up their large surveyor's tent on a spot about fifty yards from the cabin, beyond the garden. Paul, a wiry, energetic artist with thin brown hair, built a wooden floor and began assembling the tent with Colleen's help. They were both good with their hands and had the large tent up in a day, complete with cloth screening for the windows. A genuine northern Canadian bush tent, it proved a livable summer space.

Meanwhile, Steve and Shirley had brought rolls of muslin (cheaper than canvas, it could be bought by the pound) from their winter residence in Wakefield. They had already cut and waterproofed large measured pieces of the muslin in preparation for the erecting of the teepee. But first Steve had to cut the teepee poles, and the huge muslin sheets had to be sewn together.

On a fine day marking the cusp between spring and summer, with cumulus clouds in the blue sky resembling the cauliflowers we hoped would appear in the garden in August, Shirley and Steve hauled their treadle sewing machine out into the field in front of the cabin. They laid out the enormous billowing white patches of muslin on the tops of the wild buttercups and field grasses. Surrounded by the huge sheets, Shirley began to sew the sections of the teepee together, pumping the treadle steadily with her right foot, her hands passing the cloth under the heavy needle. With epic concentration and unflagging energy, she worked all day, assisted by Steve, who kept feeding the ever-growing piece of muslin through the sewing machine. Once all the muslin pieces had been sewn together into a single huge cloth, it seemed as if one of those clouds overhead had settled down gently onto the field.

At this point Steve, with my assistance, cut, stripped, and hauled seventeen long slim poles of spruce and pine out of the forest. Once these were prepared, we all assembled to help erect the teepee. The procedure felt like a ritual as we eased the first triad of poles into the sky, already tied together near the top, and spread them out as a tripod on the earth. We then added the other poles one after another, creating a large circle of poles on the ground and a small circle in the heavens. The final pole was raised with the muslin cloth already attached to it. The cloth was then unwrapped and stretched around the other poles. It was like dressing a bride for her wedding day, or wrapping a king in his royal cloak.

Where the two ends of the muslin came together was the location for the door. Above the door Steve had cut slits in the muslin. Small peeled sticks were shoved through these slits to hold the two ends of the cover together.

The architecture of a teepee is profound in its understanding of fire, smoke, wind, and weather. The previous autumn Steve had found a book on teepees advertised in the *Whole Earth Catalog* — our Bible at the Farm. He had ordered it and studied it from cover to cover. Steve read that a good teepee required an inner cover, as well, also muslin or canvas, that went up six feet or so, attached to the poles on the inside. The space between the inner and outer covers allowed airflow from outside because the outer cover didn't quite touch the ground (while the inner cover was brought right down to the earth and weighted with stones). The air moved in and up between the covers, ensuring that the smoke from the fire was drafted up through the smoke hole at the top.

Numerous other details made life livable in the teepee, at least in the summer. An underground trench was dug from the bottom of the firepit to the outside of the teepee in order to bring air directly into the pit. The system of smoke flaps, attached to two movable poles, was complex and yet, once understood, simple to use and efficient. Thought was given to how to deal with rain to guarantee the dwelling stayed dry inside with no bothersome drips from poles. Every detail in the teepee revealed a deep understanding of the earth and the heavens and how to bring them together in a harmonious way. As I watched Steve carefully adjusting the two movable poles to control the smoke hole at the top, I could tell he was in his element.

Bowing down to enter through the low-cut doorway of the teepee was itself an act in preparation for entering a sacred space. Once you were inside, the cone-like shape of the teepee amplified the songs of chickadees and whippoorwills, while leaves fluttering on nearby trees cast lively shadows on the white muslin. Twenty-two feet across, the teepee could easily sleep four or five. While sleeping in the teepee, one had the soothing feeling that one was both inside and outside, that one slept wrapped in a kind of pupa that was perfectly integrated with the natural world. Once on a midsummer night, I awoke to gaze on clusters of stars glittering in the wide-open smoke hole, as if I were inside a soft white telescope.

It was a delightful time for all of us that summer — discovering perhaps for the first time that we had some control over our world, a measure of choice over the essentials of food, water, lodging, heat, and so on. We were all artists with an abiding attraction to beauty in the world, whether it was a sunset lighting the hillside, waves of grain in a piece of wood, the radiant heartbeat of an outdoor fire, a crisp night sparkling with mica-chip stars, or a poem we shared.

Erratic North

A typical day at the height of summer — the greenery surrounding us was so thick it felt like a northern rain forest — consisted of cooking breakfast over the open firepit outside, including cowboy coffee; work in the garden or on one of the vehicles; a salad lunch picked fresh from the garden and fields; a swim at a local lake; an afternoon of writing or drawing or reading or flute playing; an evening meal again over the outdoor firepit, a bean stew richly flavoured with basil and summer savoury from the garden, or spaghetti with a primavera sauce (before we knew that's what it was called) whose vegetable contents changed every time we ate it; and ending with a long evening of conversation and beer outdoors beside the fire.

In retrospect it really was a kind of paradise that summer. We were surrounded by nature's bounty: the field in front of the cabin a rich tapestry of daisies, buttercups, chicken and eggs, devil's paintbrush, and delicate white or purple field mallows. Endless summer days were punctuated with long walks in the surrounding forest, the scent of pine needles on a hot afternoon lingering in the air. Evenings brought the smell of woodsmoke and comfortable temperatures, and finally the shimmering silk scarf of the Milky Way unfurled across the heavens.

Part 3

I
Civil War

THE WIDESPREAD REACTION AGAINST the draft during the Vietnam conflict in the 1960s wasn't the first time conscription had met with serious resistance in the United States. During the Civil War, President Abraham Lincoln decided it was necessary to implement a draft in 1863 to increase numbers in the military. Immediately, riots broke out in Boston, Newark, Jersey City, Staten Island, Williamsburg, and Troy, New York. But the most serious riots took place in New York City between July 11 and 16 of that year.

Men were drafted unless they could provide an acceptable substitute or pay $300 to buy themselves out. At the time $300 was approximately the average salary a worker could earn in one year. This class-based draft was vehemently opposed by the lower classes, especially recent Irish immigrants in New York City. The reasons for draft resistance, however, were complex. Recent Irish immigrants competed with blacks for the lowest-paying jobs and saw no reason to fight with the Union forces to end slavery in the South. The Irish worried that the cities of the North would be inundated by newly freed blacks coming to take their jobs away.

When the draft was announced, a mob of 50,000 Irish looted New York's East Side, burned a black church and orphanage, and lynched several black men. A thousand casualties and anywhere from twenty-five to one hundred deaths resulted from pitched battles with police and militia before the riots were put down. In the end, Lincoln was only able to raise 150,000 of the 300,000 draftees required, and three-quarters of those were "substitutes," that is, men paid by others to take their place. Tammany Hall, the Democratic Party machine that ruled New York City with a raised and threatening shillelagh, covered the cost of draft buyouts for many Irishmen in return for a lifetime of votes.

Erratic North

The well-known Civil War photographer Matthew Brady also had an influence on the eruption of draft riots at that time. His groundbreaking photographs of the war were limited by the technology of the day. Because exposure required several seconds' duration, shots of men in action were impossible. Posed shots were favoured, as well as the quintessential still-lifes of war: the dead, the dying, and the wounded. This provided a clear picture of a battle's aftermath, the suffering experienced by real soldiers in real war. Many of the photos were graphic, grisly, and shocking, not heroic at all. The photos were widely published in *Leslie's* and *Harper's* magazines and as etchings in numerous newspapers in 1862. The public reaction was one of shock and disgust, with the result that the next year's draft was strongly resisted.

A similar reaction met the televised images that lit the world's living rooms during the Vietnam War. The media gorged on a daily diet of wounded, dying, and dead American boys and Vietnamese civilians in jungles half a world away. People could see for themselves what the war meant for those fighting it.

The American military has learned its lesson from the public reaction to the media coverage of Vietnam. Journalists in Iraq are "embedded," which basically means "censored at source," and no photos of soldiers in pieces, or even their flag-draped coffins, are allowed. (In 2006 the newly elected Conservative government in Canada first adopted this same policy and then reversed its decision when the families of dead soldiers themselves complained.) In the United States the privacy of the soldiers' families is given as the official reason in this public-relations war over the control of images.

The New York Draft Riots were essentially a class riot — the wealthy could buy themselves out and the poor could not. Vietnam, too, had its "class" aspects. Sons of the upper classes often found a way, through connections, to avoid Vietnam and remain at home. Sons of the lower class, generally, had no recourse and had to report for duty or, in the case of many black Americans, disappear into the ghettos or go to jail. For many young people from the inner cities and from rural farming or mountain areas where poverty is endemic and generational, the military is seen as an escape from poverty or as the only means to pay for college. The phenomenon of draft resistance, especially for those who came to Canada, was, for the most part, an action taken by sons of the middle and upper middle class. Opposed to the war, these draftees voted with their feet.

2

Letterhead

I WAS A SON OF the middle class through and through. My father was a successful businessman, my mother a housewife, and a caterer in earlier years. Obtaining a university education was the focus of my schooling, as it was for both of my brothers (five and ten years older than me) and my sister (five years younger). After graduating from Loyola University in Chicago in 1969, I lived at home and worked for a year teaching elementary school in Berea, Ohio, the suburb of Cleveland where my parents lived at that time. Near the end of that school year the National Guard killed four student protestors at Kent State University on May 4, 1970, less than fifty miles away. I engaged my grade six class in lively yet serious discussions about this pivotal event. One of the other lay teachers, a middle-aged woman, at this small Catholic school told me the same day, "Those protestors got what they deserved."

After I completed my first year of teaching, the Selective Service started drafting teachers and instituted a draft lottery, the first drawing since 1942. Held on December 1, 1969, at Selective Service National Headquarters in Washington, D.C., the lottery was for men between the ages of eighteen and twenty-six. The old photos of the lottery draw resemble the set of a TV game show from the 1950s. Three hundred and sixty-six blue plastic capsules were placed in a container, one for each day of the year, including February 29. Capsules were drawn at random. Men born on any of the first 195 dates drawn were eligible for induction. The first date drawn was September 14 and the last (Number 366) was June 8, so all those born on September 14 between 1944 and 1950 were sure to be drafted. Those born on June 8 could go on with their lives. I was born on January 2, 1948, and my lottery number was 159, making me eligible. Some months later, as the bureaucratic machine turned in its inexorable drive to suck me into its gears, I received orders to report for a physical.

I reported to a high-rise in downtown Cleveland for the physical in the vain hope that someone would declare me unfit for service, but I passed with flying colours. At that point in the war they were taking just about anyone they could get: misfits, flatfoots, the half-crippled, and the half-crazed. The Land of Snow and Pierre Trudeau's smiling face beckoned.

Around this time my mother and my sister, Marilyn, who was in high school then, were attending classes on the draft, learning the facts about how to become a conscientious objector and how to go to Canada if necessary. These were held in an upstairs room of the convent connected to Lourdes Academy, my sister's all-girls high school in downtown Cleveland. The older nuns at the academy didn't want "seculars" to walk through the corridors of the convent, so the twenty or so people attending the classes, mostly nuns and mothers of draft-age boys, had to enter and leave by the fire escape. The only male at these free evening classes was the draft counsellor teaching them.

Meanwhile, the wheels of bureaucracy turned in their slow, persistent way. A letter arrived from the Selective Service System, ordering me to report for induction on March 22, 1971. Mentally, I was already in Canada. A few days later I left for good, heading back up to Toronto to stay with Albert, a university friend from Chicago who had also gone to Canada.

Once a draft resister had failed to report for induction, a warrant was issued for his arrest.

My parents did everything they could to try to convince me to stay in the United States. I recall numerous lively discussions (more like arguments, according to my sister, who had to suffer through these long, trying evenings) around the dining-room table with my parents trying to convince me to obtain conscientious objector status. At the time I couldn't imagine working in a hospital. I argued that CO status was an implied support for the war, whereas going to Canada and not reporting for the draft was a capital S statement. In any case, the Selective Service wasn't giving CO status to men raised as Roman Catholics, and I knew this. My parents never wanted me to go to war, but they preferred that I stay in the United States.

Once I was drafted and decided to go to Canada, my mother began a determined telephone and letter-writing blitzkrieg, contacting everyone she could imagine who might be able to obtain a pardon. My mother is a small woman, but her energy is boundless when it comes to reaching her goals. She gets a determined look in those intense blue-grey eyes and watch out! Senator, congressman, governor, government official — it didn't matter. She had her job to do and, by God, she would harry and cajole and plead and threaten and beg and bother until that job was accomplished. I half suspect I was eventually pardoned to get her off someone's back.

In 1973 a peace treaty was signed, ending the Vietnam War. Several years after the war ended, a letter from the Selective Service System, addressed to me, was sent to my parents' home in the suburbs of Cleveland. Entitled a "Notice of Cancellation" and dated January 8, 1975, the letter stated: "Your order to report for induction issued by this local board on March 22, 1971, has been cancelled."

I remember scratching my head and asking myself: How can something be legally cancelled four years after it was supposed to have happened? I'm glad it was, of course — it eventually allowed me to go back to the United States for visits — but still it seems like a rather extra-legal thing to do. Was this an action taken by a rogue Selective Service official, perhaps with her own son facing jail time? Was this a directive from on high, perhaps even from the president, with no public announcement? Also, was this a document that many draft resisters received or one that my mother was able to cajole for me alone? A few years later, in 1977, President Jimmy Carter announced a pardon for most Vietnam-era draft evaders.

My mother, a naturalized American citizen who was born and raised in Toronto, took it upon herself to try to determine if the "cancellation" was in fact a "pardon." Wishing to ensure that I wouldn't be arrested at the border, she talked to the office of Jerome Randolph, assistant U.S. attorney for the Northern District of Illinois (where my draft board was located, because I had registered while at university in Chicago), who told her that I didn't face prosecution for draft evasion. But my mother wanted it in writing. When a letter from Randolph wasn't forthcoming, she contacted the Midwest Central Committee for Conscientious Objectors (CCCO) in Chicago, an agency for military and draft counselling. The CCCO replied with the following letter, dated February 21, 1975:

Dear Mrs. Frutkin:

If your son Mark sends us authorization for a check of his draft file, of course we will get it done. But I really do not believe that a file check should be necessary in his case. You sent me a copy of the cancellation of Mark's induction order. And in your letter, you said that Mr. Randolph (the Asst. U.S. Attorney in charge of draft cases here) has told you that Mark does _not_ face prosecution for draft refusal.

Of course, I'm sure that you and Mark would feel better if you obtained written confirmation of the U.S. government's action in deciding not to prosecute Mark. Because Mr. Randolph is terribly overworked and cannot answer all his mail, it might prove impossible for you, or for Mark, or for me, to obtain such written confirmation from the U.S. Attorney's office. However, the U.S. Attorney's office here _will_ reply to an inquiry from a member of the U.S. Senate (or House of Representatives). So I would suggest that you have one of your Senators, or your Congressperson, write to the U.S. Attorney's office here, asking the following simple question: Was an arrest warrant or indictment charging draft refusal ever issued against your son Mark Frutkin?

If no Ohio member of Congress will co-operate with you in making such an inquiry on your behalf, ask Senator Stevenson's office here to make the inquiry for you.

If by any chance your son Mark has become a Canadian citizen, please be sure not to mention this to the member of Congress or to the U.S. Attorney. I would be glad to explain at greater length. Also, if Mark is still a U.S. citizen but is considering Canadian (or other foreign) citizenship, you might suggest that he write to us. We could give him information on the implications of foreign citizenship for his right to return to the States — and this is information he should consider carefully before making the irrevocable decision to become naturalized elsewhere.

Why did the U.S. government drop the prosecution against Mark? You almost surely will never get an official explanation. If you or Mark would tell me about his draft history, I could probably explain.

Peace,
Jeremy Mott

Approximately two weeks later, on March 7, 1975, a letter came from Adlai Stevenson's office on letterhead from the United States Senate (the title in a font that can only be described as Baroque Hysterical):

Dear Mrs. Frutkin:

Senator Stevenson has asked me to thank you for your recent letter regarding your son, Frank [sic], and to tell you that he understands your concern.

We have contacted the United States Attorney's office and requested that we be informed whether or not there is an arrest warrant outstanding for Mark. As soon as we receive a reply to our inquiry in your behalf, we will be in touch with you again.

Sincerely,
Carol Bergenstal
Staff Assistant to
Adlai E. Stevenson, U.S.S.

So now I was Frank Frutkin! My last name has been butchered repeatedly over my lifetime (a divorce lawyer once called me "Mr. Fruitbin"), but seldom has my first name been a problem. Then a letter dated May 12 arrived from Adlai Stevenson's office:

Dear Mrs. Frutkin:

Senator Stevenson is very pleased to inform you that your son Mark's name does not appear on the list of draft evaders against whom charges are presently outstanding. We have been assured by Jerome C. Randolph, Assistant U.S. Attorney for the Northern District of Illinois, that because Mark's name is not on the list, all charges against him have either been dismissed or are in the process of being dismissed.

If you have any further questions or need further assistance, please do not hesitate to call on us again, and we will be happy to help in any way we can.

Sincerely,
Carol Bergenstal
Staff Assistant to
Adlai E. Stevenson, U.S.S.

It appeared I was a free man and, theoretically, could cross borders like any other citizen of the world. Nevertheless, I was anxious about putting this theory to the test.

A few months later I made my first trip back to the United States in five years. It wasn't until I was sitting on the bus and nearing the border that I realized I only had $15 in my pocket! I was so unused to dealing with money at the Farm, and had so little of it in any case, that it hadn't occurred to me to ensure that I had a sufficient wad before crossing the border. My father was scheduled to pick me up at the bus station in Cleveland, and I already had my return bus ticket back to Ottawa, so the thought of money had never crossed my mind.

Part 3

When we pulled up to the border, the authorities took me off the bus and ushered me into the U.S. Customs office. The agent asked me how much money I had. "Fifteen dollars," I replied sheepishly.

"Fifteen dollars!" he shouted. "I can't let you into the United States with just fifteen dollars! Got any credit cards?"

I shook my head.

The agent called over his superior, who took one look at my flannel shirt and jeans and told his younger gung-ho underling to go do something elsewhere.

I tried to explain. "My father's picking me up at the bus station in Cleveland. I won't need much money while I'm there and I already have my return ticket." Turning to indicate the bus, I noticed a line of heads peering at me through the bus windows, wondering why I was delaying them. "I live on a farm and don't have much need for money."

He smiled. "I've got a small farm, too," he said. "What are you raising?"

"A few chickens, some vegetables."

We talked a little more. He stamped my passport. I got back on the bus and walked the gauntlet of the other passengers, who glared at me as I passed. I felt like a criminal. But I was a free man. Poor, but free.

Part 4

I

Wolf Lake: Spring 2004

Almost twenty-five years after I left the Farm, the 200-acre spread is still called home by a handful of the originals and a few newcomers. The original Farm has five houses on it, and the cabin still stands, although it's looking rather sad and lonely these days. Everyone else on the Farm joined together to have electricity brought in to their own houses sometime in the 1980s. I had already moved to the city, so the cabin remains the lowest of low-tech, that is, without electricity or running water.

On a gorgeous spring day in late May, I decide to take a drive from my current home in Ottawa up into the Gatineau Hills forty-two miles north to Wolf Lake. I arranged an interview with Hazel, eighty-three, who was the postmistress in the village during the period I lived on the Farm. I want to find out what Hazel remembers about Louis and Albert, the Drouin brothers, and what she might have to say about the draft resisters who I have heard lived in the hills around Wolf Lake during the Second World War.

In the 1970s the post office consisted of a small room built onto the side of her house. With its own separate entrance, this little addendum (now a pantry, she later tells me) was a warren of cubbyholes and exuded a familial warmth that included a murmur of friendly gossip. I haven't seen Hazel in twenty-five years.

As I drive up Route 5, the Autoroute de la Gatineau, a four-lane highway that climbs out of the Ottawa River valley and into heavily forested hills, I realize I am not merely out for a pleasant ride but am actually taking a journey into the past, for this road and its attenuations (105 North and 366 West) are lined with memories, and the memories of memories.

Erratic North

As Route 5 climbs north, the vista on the left, to the west, is filled with the hills of Gatineau Park, and this will hold true, with a few exceptions, for the entire trip to Wolf Lake. As the highway passes the quaint village of Old Chelsea, represented by a church spire in the distance and three or four good restaurants, I recall attending a burial there on a day of wet snow in November, the interment of my first wife's father, a man I hardly got to know before hard drinking and a tedious government job put him in an early grave. I recall it was perfect weather for a burial. The sky was appropriately sombre, grey, and leaden as a dead man's eyelids, the snow a sickly greyish-white against the rich black loam of the freshly dug grave. A few days before, my sister-in-law had appeared at the door of her family home. She had just driven up from the city to announce that their father had passed away in the hospital while she was there. I answered the knock, my wife behind me. My wife's sister had stood in the doorway, unable to speak, a bouquet of flowers from his sick room in her arms. Before she could find her voice, I heard the unmistakable cry of geese heading south for the winter, and I knew he was gone.

Past Chelsea the highway enters an area that is entirely within the park and therefore free of buildings and other man-made structures. Suddenly, one begins to get a taste of the enormous spaciousness and emptiness of Canada's northern bush country. I begin to relax, to decompress, as the city falls away behind me. On both sides of the now steeply climbing highway, the bush predominates: low rocky hills thick with spruce, pine, maple, birch, and alder; a few small swampy lakes barely visible; the brilliant blue sky above all on this particular day. This is typical Canadian Shield country. At several points the highway cuts through rock formations that reveal, with graph-like clarity, the shattered foundation of the Shield, fractured and scored in patterns and horizontal striations that suggest ice cracking under great weight. In fact, it was ice more than a mile thick that did the weighing and cracking. This country was swept clean by ice-age glaciers that took the good rich soil down into the United States and southern Ontario and left behind a world that must have looked like the surface of the moon at the time.

Part 4

The Gatineau Hills are rooted in a foundation of Precambrian igneous rock overlain by Paleozoic sedimentary deposits. These hills have been called the "roots" of mountains. On top of the foundation rock are the glacial deposits left behind like monumental bear scat as the glaciers retreated: glacial till (gravel and clay that account for the area's generally poor soil), glacial stria and, the most suggestive of all geological words, erratics, or boulders transported from their original locations and dropped at random as the ice melted. One can walk along paths in Gatineau Park and come upon erratic boulders that stand along the way in sizes ranging from small service stations of solid granite to fire hydrants, all tattooed with starbursts of lichen and moss.

The Gatineaus are at the western end of the Laurentian chain. The hills are heavily furrowed by narrow valleys and elevation ranges between 500 and 1,200 feet. The Laurentians (and thus, the Gatineaus) are considered the oldest mountains in the world. In fact, Laurentia, and North America in general, is considered the oldest continent, coherent since 1.7 Ga.

In the endlessly deep valley of geological history, Laurentia apparently was located at the equator. Those days, obviously, are long gone, because as I drive up the highway from Ottawa to Wolf Lake, I pass through three of the ten climate bands that cut across Canada, their interstices narrowing in this region. The difference in temperature between Ottawa and forty-eight miles north can be distinct, with a much shorter growing season in the hills. Around Wolf Lake one hundred frost-free days is unusual. Every growing season I was forced to replant my tomatoes, first planted in the heat of great hope at the end of May and blackened by frost in early June.

The four-lane highway ends after about six miles but not before offering a splendid high view over the Gatineau Hills rolling to the east where the Gatineau River wends its turbulent way from far in the north. The Gatineau River starts in a chain of lakes called the Baskatong Reservoir, wild country, more water than land, north of the town of Maniwaki, and flows southward, punctuated with rapids, waterfalls, and hydroelectric stations, for 234 miles until it joins the Ottawa River near the capital. The Gatineau River was the site of the invention of "river driving" of timber, first used in the 1880s by a logger named Philemon Wright, who came from Massachusetts. By floating timber down the river, trees could be cut farther north and delivered to mills downstream. In the nineteenth century much of Britain's Royal Navy was built with towering straight white pine from the Gatineaus.

At its end the four-lane expressway turns into the two-lane Route 105 that twists and swirls its way toward the village of Wakefield. This highway is considered one of the more dangerous routes in Canada, due to a nasty combination of ill-balanced curves, heavy traffic, high speed limits, lunatic Quebec drivers, and perilous winter weather. I once knew a young woman from Wakefield, a former girlfriend, who lost five of her family members in a crash along this treacherous route.

Past the Great Canadian Bungee Jump, located at the site of an abandoned quarry, the highway splits, the left fork heading north for Maniwaki. The turnoff to the right passes a brand-new funeral home and crematorium and heads down a steep hill into the pretty village of Wakefield, which lies on a wide turn in the Gatineau River, once the watery highway for vast log booms now banned.

On this trip I bypass Wakefield, the site of such a profusion of memories that, if we were to stop and visit, we would never reach Wolf Lake and the good home baking I suspect awaits me at Hazel's. (It will turn out my suspicions are correct.) At the top of the hill we take the left fork and come to a view of the highway ahead. You can see the road dipping down a hill, crossing a creek (that becomes a mill pond and waterfall in Wakefield), then climbing a long slope as a divided highway. At the base of the hill I turn left onto 366 West and head in the direction of Lac des Loups.

We have now entered the land of Québécois French Fry Folk Art. Chip wagons dot village and country landscapes throughout Quebec (and parts of Ontario, too). A standard sign for a chip stand is a large wooden box (about half the size of a typical city dumpster), wider at top than bottom, stuffed with two-by-fours painted to represent the pleasing golden brown of French fries sticking out of a cardboard carton. (Some industrious company in Quebec must sell a paint called "French fry gold.") These representations of a box of chips exhibit the highest level of folk art and can look deliciously edible. There must have been similar "signs" for hungry medieval travellers walking the pilgrimage routes throughout Europe — perhaps a boar's head or a staff of wheat to show that meat, bread, and beer were available within.

Part 4

The high point of this culinary experience was revealed to me at a tiny chip stand that opened in the heart of the village of Wolf Lake one summer when I still lived at the Farm. The stand was built of wood and wasn't much bigger than an outhouse. From the Formica counter that stood hard by the road passing through the village, the customer could look through the open rear window of the stand and see the potato field in which the potato was grown that the owner was currently passing through a hand-operated chip cutter mounted on the wall. The odour of deep-fried potatoes soon filled the air about the stand. It was for good reason that the ground before the counter was damp with drool. These were chips made in heaven for famished gods with good taste. But, alas, the stand was closed by autumn, never to open again. Maybe the chip stand never really existed but was something I dreamt one hungry August afternoon wavy with light. Maybe it blew away with the autumn geese to a special lonely village in a Québécois version of paradise.

Continuing my drive, I pass farms with rolls of hay that resemble huge green barrels on their sides, past the entrance to Lac Philippe, a bountiful swimming lake and campground in Gatineau Park, past the site of a former bar that burned down where a woman I knew once slapped me in the face (for no good reason that I can recall). I then enter the land of the many villages named Masham. The first and largest village is Ste-Cécile-de Masham, settled about 1835, with an oversize (for the size of the village) stone church at its heart, its silver tower culminating in a neon cross as if the inhabitants were intent on advertising Christ's message to any late-arriving aliens.

Ste-Cécile-de-Masham is followed by Masham Mills, on La Pêche Creek, which flows just to the east of all the Mashams, followed by St-François-de-Masham with its typical Québécois houses huddled inches from the roadway, followed by St-Louis-de-Masham where a fork in the road and a general store mark a place where the fields widen and the hills move into the distance. A short way past this split, on the right fork, one comes to a little house that has always intrigued me.

When I lived at the Farm in the 1970s, this tiny farmhouse was occupied by eight sisters, all spinsters, and one brother, a bachelor. All were in their seventies and eighties then. At times I glimpsed the elderly gentleman, standing in the open door of their toy barn, sharpening an axe or knife on a large whetstone wheel. I never saw the women out of doors. One wonders what strange tales inhabit that house still, tales we will most likely never know, and yet leave to the imagination at our peril.

What is a Masham? you may ask. It turns out there is a town of Masham in North Yorkshire in England, home of the Masham Sausage Shop, suppliers of award-winning sausage products. (There *really* is a prize for everything.) And there was a Damaris Masham (1658–1708), the first English woman to publish philosophical writings (*A Discourse Concerning the Love of God*), but I doubt if Masham, Quebec, is named after her, unless those pioneers had more of a sense of humour than formerly believed. Other than these references I have discovered no obvious source for this odd name.

I like to think that Ste-Cécile, the saint of the main Masham church, is named after Cecilia, a virgin martyr of the third century, patron saint of poets, singers, music, and musicians. I like to think I passed under her gate and guidance as I made my way out to the place where I would serve my apprenticeship as a writer. When Cecilia's church in Rome was rebuilt in 1599, they say her body was discovered to be incorrupt, although it disintegrated in the air immediately upon being unveiled, a convenient way to explain the lack of evidence, if you ask me.

Several miles along the road, after a sharp turn down a hill surrounded by bush, I pass Montée Drouin, the dirt road with grass growing down its centre that skirts my cabin. I remember the night the municipality decided to give the road a proper name. I was attending another of the scintillating municipal meetings — this one in Ste-Cécile-de-Masham — when the discussion arose. I snapped awake from my doze and listened. One councillor said, in French, "Why don't we call it Chemin Frutkin?" After a minimum of discussion, it was decided. As the mayor was about to gavel the name into existence for all posterity, one of the councillors came to his senses.

"Whoa, whoa, whoa, one minute! Frutkin? What kind of a French name is that?" A bit more discussion ensued, punctuated with quite a bit of laughter and friendly nods in my direction. While no one strenuously objected to naming the road Chemin Frutkin, the councillors decided it might be more linguistically appropriate to christen this 2.4-mile track

Chemin Drouin, or even better, Montée Drouin, after Louis, the resident who had previously lived on it. *Montée* means "climb" or "ascent" or "slope," so in English it would be called the Drouin Mountain Road or High Road. At any rate, my momentary flirt with fame was over before it began. The road was given the name Montée Drouin, and so the sign where the road meets the highway reads to this day. In a sadly ironic twist, I picture Louis, unable to read, standing beneath the sign indicating the road named after his family, wondering what it says.

I bypass the turnoff to my road, and several miles farther along the highway come to the head of Wolf Lake. On this day the lake water is startlingly bright metallic blue (the blue of Henri Matisse), brilliant, radiating sunlight from thousands of wavelets, the lake appearing brisk and fresh along its length of a mile. The road swings around to the right and follows the lake closely as it passes through the village. A combination of cottages and small permanent dwellings lines the road, and at one of these I pull into the driveway.

Hazel waves to me from the kitchen window and lets me in. With a full bush of white hair, she looks healthy for eighty-three. After twenty-five years, I still recognize her, which surprises me. She greets me kindly. "You still look the same," she says, echoing my thoughts, despite the fact that my hair is two feet shorter, considerably thinner, and greyer, and despite the addition of forty pounds around the midsection and forty more wrinkles on the face.

"That's nice of you to say," I reply.

Born of Irish parents in 1921 on the nearby Foran farm, the second of thirteen children, seven of whom died in childbirth or as infants, she was later married to a gentle Québécois woodworker with the intriguing name of Zephirin, now dead several years. On my asking, Hazel reminds me that the woman who lived in my own cabin before me was Mrs. Pierre Drouin, the Irish wife of Louis Drouin's uncle. Old Mrs. Pierre Drouin raised a variety of flowers in her garden, which she offered to the local women to take on their visitations to the Wolf Lake graveyard. "She had to walk into the village, you know — every time she wanted groceries or to get the mail, she had to walk." That was a distance of about two and a half miles, a route I knew well, having walked it many times myself.

Erratic North

This discussion about someone who lived in my house before me makes me reflect on how strange it is that the dwellings we live in are privy to the most intimate moments of our lives — lovemaking, arguments, illness, perhaps even birth and death — and yet someone else can move in the next week or month or year and have no idea of the quality of those intimacies, perhaps have no notion of who the previous tenants were. I find this intriguing — that the walls surrounding us have memories of their own of which we remain ignorant.

As we sit at the kitchen table with a view out a picture window overlooking her clipped yard shaded by well-spaced trees, Hazel shows me stacks of old photographs. Numerous family shots include two of her aunts, known as Irish twins, born at opposite ends of the same year: January 1, 1901, and December 31, 1901. We flick through the pile of black-and-white photos. A woman milks a cow out in a field. Men pull wood on sledges through the snow, boil sap in the bush. ("They sometimes worked till midnight during sapping season.") A couple sits on a horse-drawn wagon, furs on laps. (I ask, "What kind of fur? They look like rabbit." She shrugs and says, "We called them buffalos.") One photo from the 1950s shows the old schoolhouse, which was sold to a local who wanted to move the building to his lot. The structure is mounted on four flatbed trucks, one at each corner, two facing east and two facing west. They moved the school into place by the two lead trucks driving forward and those behind driving in reverse.

She recalls when she was a child that her family received visits from a small Jewish peddler (the yarmulke was the defining feature) who walked to farms throughout the countryside with a special carryall on his back for various and sundry items such as cloth and tin pots. If he arrived late in the afternoon, the family generously put him up for the night rather than allow him to sleep out of doors in this wild country. The next morning he would be on his way. Silently, I wonder if he was a long-lost relative from White Russia.

I ask if she knew Louis Drouin and his brother, Albert. She nods. "They were real good-natured. They'd do anything for you. They never went to school, though. I remember once they were at my brother's store — they were drinking in the stable beside it and coming into the store to

Part 4

talk and visit. They were nice boys, but when they drank, you know ... But they weren't the only ones like that, of course."

"You know Louis killed himself in the 1980s?" I ask.

"Oh, yes. He used the gun, eh? But he did it right in the house — they didn't have to go looking for him. The wife, though, she was in bad shape."

We talk a while longer and then she pauses. "Will you be having some lunch?"

After a meal of young raw asparagus spears from the garden, potato salad, lettuce salad, homemade buns, thick slices of ham, strawberry shortcake, and tea, I ask her about the war and the French-speaking draft resisters I've heard about in the Wolf Lake area. She thinks for a moment.

"Well, there was a camp up in the bush, about four miles from here. Everyone called it the Deserters' Camp, but I call it the Hunters' Camp. I don't like using that other name. It was near a hunting place we called 'the old woman,' don't ask me why. Four boys lived there in caves during the war. One pair of brothers hid for several years, their food brought to them by relatives. When they finally came out, the experience had been so difficult that one ended up in an asylum and the other became a drunk. Lots of people from the village fed them and sometimes the police came looking for them, but nobody said a thing. And there was also two boys from the village who went to the war and one came back wounded and died."

She's crying now, dabbing her eyes with a handkerchief she took out of her sleeve. "Oh, I'm an old crybaby." She pauses and looks out the window. "Well, when you think of it, of all the wars, what have we gained — a whole lot of lives lost, and we're still losing them. I can't see any sense to it at all."

On the road back toward Ottawa, I slow down as I pass the farm where Louis used to live. He moved to this house on the highway, his father's, long before I arrived, because it had electricity, which came to Lac des Loups in 1950. I say "this house," but there is nothing there now — the field stands empty.

After several stays in the hospital for treatment of stomach cancer, Louis took things into his own hands and committed suicide by shooting himself in the stomach with his rifle. Several years later, after his wife and children moved into the village of Wolf Lake, the local volunteer fire department decided to use the old Drouin house and all its surrounding outbuildings, including several barns and a pigsty, as a test burn. It strikes me as exceedingly strange to look at that site now where nothing remains but a few trees, the tall grass, and the wind. House gone, Louis gone, the driveway where I first met him, the handwritten sign advertising TERRAIN A VENDRE — all gone. Disappeared from the face of the earth. As if it never existed.

It's a sad place, Louis's farm. Sad and timeless.

2
Fire

I PICTURE THE FLAMES licking up through Louis's house, igniting the grey weathered wood in his barn and pigsty, burning it all thoroughly until nothing remains but smoke, and then even that dissolves into the air, into the vastness of the bluenothing sky.

To live is to burn, our portion of candle shrinking down day by day. In the country one is much more intimate with fire than in the city, especially if one heats and cooks with it, and needs a coal-oil lamp or candles in order to see while cooking, washing up, or reading at night. A controlled fire is a necessity in the country, of course, but gazing into the firebox on bitter winter nights can also provide a feeling of home and security. And all summer, as we sat outside around the pit on long evenings watching the flames lick and the logs spit, it seemed each fire had its own distinct personality.

Fire had its sinister, wild side, as well. Every winter my hands and fingers collected a selection of burns from cooking on the wood stove. It always intrigued me how an old burn, no longer felt, hurt again when it neared the heat, as if the skin itself had retained the memory of fire within in.

Part 4

A chimney fire is not an uncommon event in the country. One windy March morning I experienced a fire that almost burned down the cabin. Janet, my first wife (we married in 1977), and I had risen and dressed. I built a fire in the wood stove, which was sucked immediately into the chimney by the powerful draft. I recall there was a roaring sound in the pipes as the fire ignited the tarry soot inside.

I ran outside and saw flames shooting out the top of the chimney as well as a plume of thick black smoke. The situation was worsened by the fact that the cabin didn't have a real brick chimney but simply lengths of thin metal stovepipe fitted together. In several places the pipes came dangerously close to the wood structure of the cabin — where they passed through the ceiling and floor above the wood stove, for example — and the wood in these areas started to smoke. Janet and I grabbed buckets of water, ran upstairs, and began soaking down all the hot spots. Having to run to the spring for more water slowed us, but fortunately the stovepipes didn't melt or fall apart and the fire eventually burned itself out. The cabin survived.

Disassembling and cleaning the metal stovepipes one by one had always been a dirty, daylong job that I resisted as long as possible. After this experience, I made a point to clean them on a regular basis.

In my years at the Farm I only saw one forest fire. It wasn't a raging inferno, as one sees every summer on the TV news from California or western Canada, but a single, slow-burning, undulating line that crawled along the hills to the west. It was autumn, the leaves had already fallen, and the forest floor was damp. The fire never left the ground, never rose into the trees, but burnt in a wavering arc, a fine line on the hillside in the distance. I first noticed it about eight o'clock in the evening, burning in a direction roughly west to east, heading straight for the Farm and my cabin. Every twenty minutes I would go outside to check on it — it was still there, edging along, a strange glowing snake in the darkness of the hills. By morning it was gone, never to be seen again.

Fire can take on many forms. One night, in the darkness of the cabin, I rose from bed and went downstairs to urinate in the field under the river of the Milky Way, hoping as always that I might see a shooting star (known to the alchemists as "celestial flowers"). As I approached the cabin's front door to step outside, I looked at the wood box where I noticed a weird glow, like moonlight. Going to the nearest window, I pulled the curtain, expecting the moon to be shining in, but there was no moon. Another glance at the wood box brought the realization that I was witnessing phosphorescence, decaying wood that gives off light. In ten years of cutting, stacking, and burning several mountainsides' worth of logs, it was the only time I experienced this phenomenon. A strange form of light without heat.

When I finally stepped outside, there was a display of aurora borealis in the heavens. On many occasions over the years at the Farm, I saw northern lights. Usually, they took up a corner of the sky and proceeded to shoot in pale, coloured shafts from the horizon upward. Several times, however, I viewed displays that were sustained, silent fireworks of light in motion. Once, they consisted of wide bands of light that twisted back upon themselves in layers, as if drapes or curtains, or sculpted robes on a Greek statue, with multicoloured waves shooting up into the sky.

On another occasion the northern lights filled the entire dome of the heavens. In every direction I looked, light flowed up continually from the full 360 degrees of horizon into the firmament. I walked out and stood in the middle of the field in front of my cabin. It was early autumn, the night not too cool. The entire sky was in motion, lines of light shooting straight up and curving in as if the sky were an inverted bowl. In the crown of the heavens, in the fontanel of the sky, the light writhed and swirled in an extraordinary display of intense activity.

The aboriginal peoples say that aurora borealis is the voices of ancestors speaking to us and there exists a distant etymological connection between the words *aurora* and *auspicious*. I wondered what the ancestors were trying to tell us.

Part 4

3
Norman Morrison

A man stands at a window in a government building in Arlington, Virginia, near Washington, D.C., in November 1965. Confused, he stares at a fire on the steps of the Pentagon. Could that be? Is it? My God ...

FIRE WAS A PRIME image and symbol of the Vietnam War. A jungle burns with napalm; a naked nine-year-old Vietnamese girl runs down the road toward the camera screaming in pain from her burns, the trees in the distance behind her still smoking; a monk is seated in meditation posture as flames consume his unmoving form. These were some of the images behind Marshall McLuhan's statement, "The war in Vietnam was lost in the living rooms of the nation."

Although most North Americans of a certain age will recall the TV images of Buddhist monks setting themselves on fire during the Vietnam era, few will recall that eight Americans also burned themselves to death in opposition to the war. They don't remember because these home-fired self-immolations weren't filmed (perhaps they were censored or no news media were present) and so they never appeared on TV screens. Nevertheless, eight Americans felt strongly enough to set themselves afire.

The man staring out the window of the government building in Washington was Robert Strange McNamara, U.S. secretary of defense at that time. He was watching a Quaker named Norman Morrison burn to death on the steps of the Pentagon on November 2, 1965. Morrison had brought his eighteen-month-old daughter with him that day — she was left safely nearby and was untouched by the flames when he immolated himself. Norman Morrison, the father of three children, had been deeply affected by reports from Vietnam of the children burnt from napalm manufactured in the United States and hoped, in his own way, to shock Americans out of their complacency in accepting this.

Norman Morrison wasn't the first American to set himself on fire. The previous March an eighty-two-year-old woman, Alice Herz, immolated herself on a Detroit street corner. Herz, who also had Quaker connections, sacrificed herself to protest the arms race around the world. The notes she and Morrison left behind depict people of sound mind who were offering themselves as martyrs in an attempt to end the war and the suffering. One week after Morrison's death Roger LaPorte, a twenty-two-year-old Catholic Worker, immolated himself in protest outside the United Nations building in New York City. Horribly burned, it took him thirty-three hours to die. Five years later George Winne, another war protestor, died from self-immolation in California.

America, like Vietnam itself, now had its moral witnesses, those who were willing to pay the ultimate price to try to end the war. Yet most Americans considered these people to be crackpots. The media chose, for the most part, to ignore these stories or provided minimal coverage.

Norman Morrison's daughter, Emily, who was brought as an infant to the Pentagon that day, wrote years later: "No matter what could have happened to me, I believe I was purposefully with my father to symbolize the tragedy and brutality of war. Because I lived, perhaps I symbolized hope as well."

The role of the Quakers (also known as the Society of Friends) in these self-immolations is intriguing. The Quakers were active in the antiwar movement, advising young men about the draft through such agencies as the Central Committee for Conscientious Objectors (the agency that corresponded with my mother).

Not a borderline sect or a cult but one of the founding Protestant denominations of the United States, Quakers settled before the Revolutionary War in Rhode Island, North Carolina, New Jersey, and Pennsylvania. William Penn, a Quaker who founded Pennsylvania, intended that the colony be a haven for Quakers and an experiment in religious tolerance. Quakers spoke of the "natural rights" of people, an idea later incorporated into the Declaration of Independence in 1776. A number of concepts that were later enshrined in the U.S. Constitution first appeared in an earlier document written by William Penn in 1682. This document, the Pennsylvania Frame of Government, promised

Part 4

freedom of speech, freedom of worship, trial by jury, and an assembly elected by the people.

Quakers believe that the divine light within the individual is the true source for guidance. Guidance can't come from external rites or intermediaries — it is the individual conscience that should guide human behaviour.

In one of history's tragic ironies, Richard Nixon was a Quaker.

4
Sweat

AT THE START OF the second summer at the Farm we decided to build a sweat lodge at the bottom of the field in front of my cabin. A sweat lodge is a traditional aboriginal sauna still used today by Native people.

Paul and Steve had taken on the job of building the sweat lodge. They began by cutting alder saplings and stripping the branches and leaves off, then bending them into a little circular hut, using wire to hold the poles together at the crown. On top of this, they stapled heavy clear plastic sheeting in order to enclose the entire hut. Finally, we covered it with whatever we could find: blankets, tarps, an old sleeping bag. Nothing elegant, but it would prove its utility soon enough.

Ten feet from the hut we built a bonfire and placed a couple dozen stones in it, ranging in size from one to three fists. We had read that one should be careful not to use rocks from a streambed as they could explode when under heat. After a couple of hours, when the fire died down and the stones were sufficiently heated, we removed them, one or two at a time, with a pitchfork. The separated tines of the fork allowed the coals to fall back into the fire as we lifted the stones and carried them to a pit that had been dug in the centre of the sweat lodge itself. Any coals or bits of wood that accidentally found their way into the pit inside would fill the lodge with choking, astringent smoke. Once the stones had been placed inside the lodge, the half-dozen of us present stripped naked and crawled into the hut with a bucket of water. The last one in drew the door shut by pulling down the plastic sheeting and a blanket. In the pitch-dark and overheated silence, the sweating began.

The aboriginal peoples consider the sweat lodge a ritual ceremony with spiritual significance. Every aspect has its meaningful symbols in relation to the natural world: the hut that resembles the bowl of heaven, the fire, the stones, the water to splash on them, sitting on the earth in a circle in the dark, sweating out that which has been soiled, emerging anew as if reborn. We never prayed to the Great Spirit, but there was something deeply cleansing about it, and more than in a physical sense.

The person closest to the bucket threw water on the hot stones, and the little hut filled with scorching steam as we sweated like commuters on a subway in July. The darkness was all-encompassing. Latecomers entering couldn't see who was already inside, or who was seated where in the circle. We became disembodied voices gathered together in a kind of pre-birth darkness, in a chthonic mist, one pool of sweat, all equal under the sun that was still shining out there somewhere.

It was extremely claustrophobic, intensely hot, and not entirely pleasurable. At the moment when we could no longer take the heat, we would jump out from the lodge, pour a bucket of cold spring water over our heads, and stand steaming in sunlight. *Like angels*, they say in aboriginal descriptions of the sweat lodge. After a sweat, one felt remade, emptied out, reborn.

My experience with the sweat lodge, a temporary structure, had convinced me that a more permanent structure for sweats and saunas would be an excellent addition to the Farm. One autumn, in the early years, Shirley, who had moved away, came for a short visit and together under the bright burning leaves we built a sauna out of cedar logs.

The Finns, the source of sauna culture, are fond of relating the health advantages of saunas: a sauna speeds up the heartbeat, improves breathing and circulation, raises body temperature, and can temporarily lower blood pressure. It can also pique the appetite and turns a cold beer into ambrosia.

Part 4

While I wasn't immune to those advantages, the sauna served a more practical function. It was an easy way to get clean in an environment where bathing was often problematic. In summer, for bathing, one could always go for a swim to a nearby lake or take a penis-shrivelling dip in the icy stream, or even bathe in a hot-weather downpour as it ran off the roof of the cabin. But bathing during other seasons proved more difficult. For years I would bathe during winter in a square aluminum tub set on the floor of the kitchen, right next to the wood stove. I would haul several extra buckets of water to the cabin and fill my huge kettle, which then heated up while I cooked dinner. After dinner, I poured cold water into the aluminum tub and added hot water from the kettle until the bath reached the right temperature. Then I stripped and stepped in. I'm not sure if that's how the pioneers did it, but it worked. Sometimes it was just easier to get together for a sauna.

When it came to building the log sauna, Shirley and I used a bucksaw to cut good-size cedar trees in an area of the cedar swamp near the stream. I had chosen what I imagined to be a perfect site for the sauna, next to a wide bend in the stream where it turned ninety degrees to the east and the current bellied out into a pool edged with sand. Together we lifted the logs stripped of leaves and branches onto our shoulders and lugged them to the site. There we notched the logs and fitted them together, the larger cedars at the bottom.

It was the simplest of structures — about six feet by ten feet. We built a rough floor out of planks and a couple of benches, one above the other, the bottom one deeper than the top so it would be easy to climb up and so those sitting on the upper seat had a place to put their feet. Wherever possible we used slab wood — the first outer cut of a log that included the bark with a bit of the actual wood. Local mills sold slab wood as cheap firewood, but we also used it to build a variety of funky structures around the Farm, including back porches, outhouses, and woodsheds. We slapped a roof on the sauna and cut a hole for the stovepipe, which protruded from a forty-five-gallon drum resting on its side in a bed of sand inside the sauna. The purpose of the sand was to keep the drum from rolling and to insulate it from the wood floor underneath. This oversize, makeshift stove, with a hole at one end for feeding the fire and another hole cut in the top to fit the pipe, served as a means to heat the stones. On one curving side of the drum we stacked the stones and stretched wire mesh over to hold them in place.

Raised as a farm girl, Shirley was a good work partner, saying little but doing her share. She appeared to be as strong as me but offered the added advantage of being a woman and therefore unlikely to make me feel like an idiot when I slammed the hammer into my thumb or wasn't able to figure out some arcane bit of carpentry wisdom which, it appeared, most guys were born understanding. Not me. I was still trying to figure out which way a nut turned on a bolt despite several years of working ceaselessly on the cabin and my decrepit cars. I was so poor — and so determined not to waste anything — that I pulled nails from old boards, straightened them, and reused them. Understandably, this was looked upon as slightly mad by the other men on the Farm, several of whom had actually attended carpenter school. (In the 1980s, young people started calling hippies "carpenters" for good reason.) Somehow, between the two of us, we managed to build the sauna and make it stand. We hung a door and stepped back to inspect our creation — a beautiful little hut nestled in a glade of trees alongside the clear-flowing stream. Basic, nothing fancy.

The first time we used the new sauna it was early spring. Patches of snow still littered the shaded areas in the forest, but the hot spring sun and the quick thaw had turned the little stream from a four-foot-wide, two-foot-deep rivulet into a raging, slick python of water coursing down from the hills and spilling over into the fields it edged. This spring version of the stream was eight feet wide — fifteen at the turn by the sauna — neck-deep, numbingly cold, and flowing fast. The six of us who had gathered together — Shirley, Steve, Paul, Colleen, Jochen, and me — set our firewood in the sauna and quickly undressed, hanging our clothes and towels on nearby trees. I lit the first ceremonial newspapers under some cedar kindling, and soon a fire was roaring inside and the stones began to heat up. Naked, we sat in rows like chickens in a henhouse. It was soothingly dark but not totally black like the sweat lodge. We relaxed as the cool of an early

Part 4

spring day left our bones and we started to sweat. Someone had picked a few branches of white birch with starbursts of young leaves, and with these we slapped each other's backs.

Typically, in the sauna, there were outbursts of chatter followed by long periods of primal silence, as the world and all its tensions fell away and dissolved and as the heat penetrated our cores. I splashed water on the hot stones, and steam hissed into the space, but only for a moment as the air was now so hot that the steam vanished almost instantly. And still we sat, melting and burning, as the heat grew slightly painful. We knew we had to climb a long slope up a mountain of heat and then immerse ourselves in the volcano's fires before we could consider leaping into the stream of liquid ice outside the sauna door.

After half an hour of delicious torture inside the sauna, I began pouring more water on the stones, which now were white-hot. The steam arose as if from a witch's cauldron as the air grew hotter and hotter and hotter still. We thought we were going to explode with heat, and the silences were miles deep as we each contemplated alone the thin edge between pain and pleasure. Finally, with a yelp and a series of trailing screams, we blew the door open and all six of us poured out and leaped into the stream.

The smooth iciness of the water couldn't touch us. Like slick otters, we ducked our heads under and let the frigid water run off our long hair. We stayed in the stream until we felt the cold start to penetrate. The contrast of extreme heat and extreme cold was profoundly energizing and certainly not recommended for anyone with a heart condition or over the age of forty.

Once we began to feel the icy waters clutching at us, we climbed from the flow and stood in the field at the stream's edge in a state of pure, physical euphoria, steam rising off us as if we were rock stars stripped naked and standing in a nimbus of dry ice.

5
Apprenticeship

Before enlightenment, chop wood, carry water.
After enlightenment, chop wood, carry water.

— Wu Li

I LEARNED TO WRITE by writing, and found there was no greater joy than sitting in front of my cabin on a spring morning with a cup of coffee in hand, a notebook on my lap, and a poem brewing in my head. I sat in the young grass itself or on a homemade wooden bench, a few daffodils starting to blossom next to me, their yellow blooms resplendent against the age-darkened logs of the cabin. Or I would take a long walk up the mountain and return with a line or two of precisely measured words, like stones set in a row.

While at the Farm during the 1970s, I immersed myself in writing and reading and in this way served my first apprenticeship, "finding my legs," as it were, in the forests of language, and beginning, just beginning, to find my own small path through that dense thicket.

During this apprenticeship, I studied with many masters. I spent long winter evenings reading novels and poetry and filling notebooks with quotes that struck me as insightful, or writing poems, almost all of which were influenced by the natural world surrounding me. (The renowned Polish journalist and author, Ryszard Kapuściński, has written: "The spinning of tales is almost unimaginable without a fire crackling somewhere nearby, or without the darkness of a house illuminated by an oil lamp or a candle.") I read the classics and the popular, but mostly I read "good literature": *Moby-Dick*, William Shakespeare, Dante's *Divine Comedy*, volume after volume of Joseph Conrad, Walt Whitman, James Joyce (Samuel Beckett came later), Lawrence Durrell, tales of Aladdin, numerous modern Japanese novels, and collections of ancient Chinese poetry. I remember being particularly taken with *One Hundred Years*

Part 4

of *Solitude* by Gabriel García Márquez, Jorge Luis Borges's *Ficciones*, Franz Kafka's short stories, and Yukio Mishima's first novel, *The Sound of Waves*.

I fell in love with Kenneth Rexroth's translations of Tang Dynasty Chinese poets. Their work struck me as astoundingly fresh and alive after more than a thousand years, imbued with the natural world and man's small place in it. The poetry had the added attraction of reflecting my own sojourn in the country.

One book that had a profound effect on me in these years was *Zen Mind, Beginner's Mind* by Shunryu Suzuki, a Japanese Zen Buddhist monk who moved to California in the 1960s. Reading this book was for me the beginning of a lifetime of study and practice in Buddhism in its Tibetan and Zen versions. Every morning in winter as I arose I started the fire and read from the book while standing next to the wood stove in my coat and boots, waiting for the cabin to warm up: "When you do something, you should burn yourself completely, like a good bonfire, leaving no trace of yourself."

His message was as simple as a cup of tea and linked intimately with the natural world. To begin a life of meditation and study on the Buddhist path is called "entering the stream" (our experience at the sauna came to mind). Little did I know the stream would turn ninety degrees and carry me down to the vast blue sea.

One day at the Farm, after a few difficult weeks of soul-searching, I decided to burn everything I had ever written. I felt my own writing and my obsession with it had become a crushing weight. I gathered together a pile of notebooks and papers — work that included everything I had ever written — took the stack out to the firepit in the yard, and started the process of annihilation. Slowly, I worked my way through the three-foot pile one page at a time. As paper turned into flame, I felt the weight lift from me. After an hour, there was nothing left but a small heap of white ash. All those colourful words had turned into a blank, illegible whiteness.

The next day I took the idea of annihilation a step farther, deciding to head out to the highway to hitchhike with absolutely no destination in mind. I left my wallet with all my identification at the cabin, intending never to return. I wanted to begin anew, to start over, to become someone else. As I strode across a field to reach the highway — taking nothing with me but the clothes on my back — Paul and Colleen's little dog, Jessie, picked up my scent and followed me. I told her to go home. She persisted. I walked on. She kept with me.

"Go home!" I shouted.

The little dog looked at me with her gentle eyes — and kept following. Finally, I decided to take it as a sign. I couldn't lead her out onto the highway where she could become lost or be struck by a car. I turned around and took her home and went back to my cabin. In a few days I began writing again. Six months later I burned everything again. Another small pile of white ash.

A few weeks later, once again I started, with a single letter — one word, one word at a time. I guess I couldn't help myself.

6
Numbers

THE NUMBERS THEMSELVES SPEAK of a military machine that was in serious trouble. Between 1960 and 1973, 503,926 members of the U.S. armed forces deserted in opposition to the Vietnam War. Strangely enough, this is close to the number of deserters in Napoleon's disastrous Russian Campaign, an astounding number of deserters for a modern army. Add to this, however, what the government itself later admitted were hundreds of thousands of draft dodgers, many of whom came to Canada. (Sweden also was a favourite destination.) The number of draft resisters who came to Canada was somewhere between 50,000 and 200,000, although hard numbers are impossible to find. An article by Robert Fulford in the *National Post* in 2001 stated that there were 50,000 Vietnam-era draft resisters and that half have since returned to the United

Part 4

States. He finds these numbers in a book by John Hagan, an "expert" on draft dodgers, but it remains unclear how Hagan arrived at his count.

In addition, there were a significant number of draft-age men who never registered, especially among black Americans. Estimates of the number of non-registrants range from 250,000 to two million. Few of these were ever tried, let alone convicted. The majority merely dissolved into new rural communities or disappeared in the massive urban ghettos of the United States. The difficulty the armed forces faced can be seen in the figures reported by the induction centre in Oakland, California, from October 1969 through March 1970. More than half of those ordered to report for induction failed to show up, and of those who did appear, 11 percent refused induction. While this might not have been a typical induction centre, nonetheless the figures must have been alarming to those responsible for finding more bodies to throw into the war. The war was widely rejected at the time by many Americans, although a slim majority of the public apparently still voiced their support (if the polls can be believed). Meanwhile, those who were expected to give up their lives for what they considered a spurious reason were making their own decisions and "voting with their feet."

The widespread resistance to the war was certainly fed by the antiwar movement. The first antiwar march in Washington, D.C., in December 1964 drew 25,000 people. Nevertheless, it was called the largest antiwar demonstration in American history up to that point. Five years later an antiwar march in New York City drew over a million participants. Burning of draft cards became a highly publicized feature event at these marches. In April 1967, at a huge peace rally in Central Park in New York City, 175 men burned their draft cards. All over the country young men were turning their cards in or burning them. On October 3, 1967, 1,500 men returned their cards in the largest single mass resistance.

Meanwhile, the country began to face opposition to the war from returning veterans. In 1967 Vietnam Veterans Against the War was formed. Disabled veterans began to appear at antiwar marches on crutches or in wheelchairs, bringing home to the American public the reality of Vietnam. The war was hitting a peak of unpopularity.

Erratic North

The war was lost in the fields, jungles, and paddies of Vietnam, but it was also lost at home. Individuals who stood up and spoke out or who simply declined to take part played a significant role in ending the war. Hundreds of thousands simply said, "No."

On May 12, 1970, a soldier named Keith Franklin was killed in Vietnam. He had written a letter that was only to be opened in the event of his death. It read:

> If you are reading this letter, you will never see me again, the reason being that if you are reading this I have died. The question is whether or not my death has been in vain. The answer is yes. The war that has taken my life and many thousands before me is immoral, unlawful and an atrocity ... I had no choice as to my fate. It was predetermined by the war-mongering hypocrites in Washington. As I lie dead, please grant my last request. Help me inform the American people, the silent majority who have not yet voiced their opinions.

Part 5

1
Fencelines and Potatoes

I'M WALKING THE FENCELINE of the Farm with Louis. He came to my cabin, as he promised, to lead me through the bush and point out the eastern border of the Farm. We're hiking through thick shaded forest, up and down craggy mounds strewn with loose, lichen- and moss-coated rock scattered like broken pottery. The aged fence consists of a tilting post about every twenty feet and two strands of heavy wire connecting one post to the next. A few slivers of sunlight filter down through the tall pines, spruce, and maples. We start at the southeast corner of the Farm and head roughly northward along the fenceline, Louis in front, me following behind.

In the thick woods he appears to be in his element. Seemingly half-bear, half-man, he says almost nothing, merely notes each post as we come to it. He does this by placing his hand on it and then moving on. He doesn't walk, he lumbers, never stumbling, each step in weighty yet intimate contact with the earth. It takes about an hour to walk the line, and he hasn't spoken two sentences, hasn't smiled. He's not unfriendly. He just has nothing to say and is focused on the job at hand. He reveals no sense of hurry, no sense that he must rush back to feed the horses or cut the hay, although I know the work never ends for him. When we are done, he doesn't linger for small talk but turns and walks back to his own farm.

As I watch Louis walk away, his profound sense of silence lingers with me. There is nothing left but a phoebe calling its own name by twos in the distance and the sound of the wind through leaves high on the hillside. This, I realize, is how a man who has spent years in the bush lives and breathes and walks. This is how someone lives who is in constant, unrelenting connection with the earth, someone who has one foot in the tamed world and another still in the wild. We live next door to each other on this land, but we live in different worlds, in different times. The medieval and the postmodern have met and don't yet know what to say to each other.

On the first warm spring day, Shirley, Steve, and I are walking down Louis's long dirt driveway. We have stopped by to reconnect after the long, lonesome winter. Louis comes out from behind his barn as we approach. He wears his sober face, but his mood lightens when I introduce Shirley. He doesn't exactly smile, but a heaviness leaves his eyes. Her arrival has brought out his magnanimity, and he will become a gentleman farmer in her radiant blond presence, revealing his version of earthbound ebullience. Near to where we stand in the drive a pair of full-grown pigs wallows in the deep caramel mud of the sty. He shows them off to Shirley by throwing the pigs a couple of half-rotten apples. The animals are enormous, their skin tight and distended by their swollen girth as they step through the muck and gobble the apples. He is proud of their size, their healthiness, even the ripe smell of life they give his farmyard.

"Big ones," Shirley, the farm girl, notes.

"*Oui.*" He nods proudly.

We chat for a few moments about the loveliness of the spring day, and he manages a pun in English about *spring* above (the season, the weather) and *spring* below (as in a water source). I have never seen him so ebullient when not drinking. He seldom takes his eyes from Shirley. His gaze is not at all aggressive but contains a significant element of shyness.

"Come. Look." Louis leads the three of us into his house and down to the cellar. He is avid to show us something. Walking to a corner of the basement, he points into a wooden crib a quarter filled with potatoes. His feeling of pride is palpable. He picks up a large, gnarled potato and hands it to Shirley. Picks up another and hands it to Steve.

"Good-looking potatoes," Shirley says. Steve and I nod in agreement.

"*Oui.* Potatoes enough to last to summer. Keep good here." He indicates the immense cellar.

"Yes, a good cellar," Shirley agrees.

Part 5

He takes the potatoes back from us and tosses them into the bin. Show and tell is over.

Out in the driveway he doesn't bother with the niceties of leave-taking. By the time we reach the end of the drive, he is already on his way to the barn with two buckets of water for the horses. He doesn't look our way, doesn't stop to wave goodbye. As he passes the sty, the pigs rush up to the fence excitedly, snorting and squealing. He ignores them, too.

2

Water

IN A MARC CHAGALL–LIKE reverie, I picture young Simon the day before he left Borisov for America. I see him going to the river to talk to his father, who had died when Simon was young (somewhere between the age of two and six). Simon believes he has glimpsed his father there several times before, deep in the water, head upside down.

"*Shalom aleichem*, Father. Father, why are you not buried in the ground like all our other ancestors?"

Simon's father turns his head in the water and looks up past his own feet. "I don't know — I guess it had something to do with my mercurial personality."

"Mercurial? What does that mean?"

"Never mind." He pauses. "Maybe your mother had me thrown in the river because it was cheaper than burying me."

"I don't know. She never said. What's it like down there, Father?"

"Lots of dead French soldiers from long ago. Other than that, well, you know … It's lonely. The fish don't talk much."

On hearing the clunk of a boat in the nearby reeds, Simon raises his head. The sounds, he thinks, on the river, on water, always so clear and crisp. The sounds on the great sea must be a million times sharper. He looks down again. "Mother wants me to take the candlesticks when I go to America."

"The candlesticks? Those came from *my* mother!"

"I told her I won't take them."

"Good."

"I leave tomorrow."

"I know."

Simon waits for some words of wisdom, a final thought to send him off. Nothing is forthcoming. "Do you have anything to say, Father?"

"There's a three-ruble note hidden under a board in the kitchen. It's for you. May you travel with *mazal* [luck]. Wait. I almost forgot. Remember this: All is written in water. Time is written in water."

"I should think time is written in the wind, as they say."

"Arguing with me? Words of wisdom I'm trying to give you. Can you not just listen? So like your mother; always were." He pauses. "Tell her I miss her. *Aleichem shalom.*"

3
Border Country

SIMON AND HIS BROTHER, Sam, a year older, walk through the woods of western Belarus, following a man who is guiding them to the border. Simon gives this man all the money that is hidden under the torn scraps of Yiddish newspaper that pad his left shoe. Back in Borisov, he was told how to find the man's hut and that this hunter would show them the path across the border and a shallow place to ford the river. This silent man will lead them out of Russia — for a price.

Under the newspapers padding his other shoe, Simon has hidden enough money to pay for his train ticket from a town near the border to the port of Hamburg and for passage to America. Sam has his own money in his own shoes. It was good they left Borisov at the end of summer because the apples in the orchards are ripe then. These have proven a supplement to their meagre provisions.

Part 5

For much of the journey the boys hitch rides on local wagons, but at this point they are forced to walk. Simon loves to walk. He is only five feet five inches and stocky, but he seems to march rather than walk, with a long stride, usually swinging his arms. Although in this case he is unable to swing his arms freely since he carries a sack that contains all his earthly goods. His complexion is dark and his eyes liquid black.

When Simon told his mother he was planning to leave for America, she fainted dead away. Simon's oldest brother, Abram, had already gone. In fact, every one of Simon's ten siblings, male and female (he was the tenth of eleven), ended up emigrating, except the youngest, a daughter. She stayed in Russia because she had married at age sixteen and was expecting a child.

With the astounding number of Jews leaving Belarus and other parts of Russia, it was as if the traditional *shammes* who walked through the streets of a town's Jewish quarter late on Friday afternoon shouting "Jews to the bathhouse!" had changed his cry to "Jews to the New World!"

Simon hadn't actually been drafted yet. Typically, the Friday evening Sabbath dinner included an *oyrekh*, a stranger as guest for the meal, and quite often this guest would be a Jewish conscript posted to their town, far from home and family. An unhappy young Jewish soldier in their presence, answering endless questions about his difficult experiences in the czar's army, would certainly have had a powerful and lasting effect on the boys in the household. After the meal, all present symbolically washed their hands with a few drops of water. Then the knives, symbols of bloody weapons, were covered with cloth and removed from the table. This was followed by the *zmiros*, placid songs of peace and contentment. Many of the rituals of the Jewish Sabbath, it seemed, worked against the military mentality.

At that time steerage passage to the United States cost about $30. Where had Simon and his brother found the money? It is likely that the relatives they were going to join in America had provided some assistance. Perhaps Simon sold vegetables or chanterelle mushrooms he picked in the forest, helping his mother from her pushcart. Perhaps they even had help from other *shtot bruders* (town brothers) in the New World. In any case, the money was found.

There was plenty of inspiration to leave Russia: recent pogroms against Jews, the czar's draft, the limitations of life in the Pale, the inability for Jews to advance in the world. The official edicts concerning Jews would be eased one year, then tightened again several years later. It was always difficult to predict what might happen next. In the 1880s the policy of providing education for everyone was countermanded. Suddenly, for Jews living within the Pale, only 10 percent were allowed to attend secondary school. The government actually sent officials to Jewish homes to measure the noses of children, and anyone with too long a nose couldn't attend school. In May 1882 the Temporary Laws (the name alone gives one the feeling that decisions were subject to arbitrary change) determined that Jews could live only in small towns and villages, that they were no longer allowed to farm or work in industry.

Simon's mother might have given her blessing to the boys' plans after learning that relations and other people from Borisov were awaiting them in America and that they would help them on arrival. In fact, Simon had written to several distant cousins in Boston and Cleveland, and others with his own family name, letting them know they would arrive sometime in the autumn.

The guide leads Simon and his brother on through a thick forest that is more shadow than light. For all Simon knows, the man is leading them straight to the czar's soldiers, from whom he will likely collect another payment. But Simon has no choice — he must trust this man.

They walk through typical Belorussian forests of beech, pine, and birch, sometimes following a discernible path, other times seeming to walk an invisible trail through stands of tall trees. The ragged openings in the leaves that reveal patches of sky look to Simon like holes in an old overcoat. Are they afraid? Yes, and excited. Out in the world, trusting a stranger to take them over a border they have never before crossed. They try to step on soft moss and avoid the cracking sticks.

Dusk comes late in that country. Eventually, they see a fast-moving river through the trees. They hear the faint barking of dogs in the distance.

Part 5

Wading across the river, the boys enter another country for the first time. Without realizing it, as they enter the water, they are ritually washing themselves in preparation for a new life.

4
Hamburg to Boston

SIMON AND SAM SIT on the train as it *clackity-clacks* through forests and fields, heading for the city of Hamburg, the world's busiest port, New York being the second busiest at the time.

At long last the train chugs into Hamburg station and comes to a stop. Simon and Sam go in search of a sign with a Star of David on it that they were told they would see in the station — a sign beneath which will be standing a helpful Jewish girl from one of the prominent Jewish charitable societies. After a short hunt, they find her, and when ten or twelve more migrants gather beneath her sign, she leads the scruffy, wide-eyed parade to the port and the ship they will take to the New World.

When they arrive at the port, they enter a building near the ship and are told to sit on benches. A woman comes into the room and tells them in Russian (those who know Russian translate it into Yiddish for the others) to remove their clothes. Once undressed they are ushered into the next room where a huge kettle boils on an iron stove. There they are sprayed with noxious clouds of carbolic soap in order to disinfect them. Meanwhile, their clothes are dusted with disinfectant powder.

The orders come as shouts: "Stop now!" "Do this!" "Go there!" "Quick!" After being showered and rinsed with hot water, they hear the order "Get dressed!" Even dressed, their skin still stinks of oil and their clothes reek of disinfectant.

Finally, they pay their fare. Their papers are checked and tickets stamped, and they board the ship with the other passengers. The crowd buzzes as the boat throbs into life and lurches away from the dock. Everyone is glued to the rails, watching the Old World disappear in the grey distance.

———

The immigrants' greatest worry was that the customs agents in America would quarantine them on one of the islands outside Boston's harbour. An outbreak of cholera and typhus in New York City in 1892 had led to widespread quarantining of immigrants.

The spread of typhus was usually fostered by the filthy conditions onboard ship. Simon and his brother rode in steerage, which had three compartments: one for single men, one for single women, and a third for families. Each compartment consisted of two rows of berths facing each other across a narrow central dining area with long wooden tables. At the end of each compartment stood a small table holding a basin filled with salt water. This was used for personal washing as well as for rinsing dishes and utensils. The toilets consisted of open troughs occasionally flushed out with buckets of salt water.

The boys, like the other passengers, ate nothing but black bread (somewhat fresh on the first day and growing more and more stale, and finally mouldy, as the journey progressed); half-decayed herring; potatoes stinking of rot; and rusty tankards of weak, tepid tea. None of the food was kosher.

Onboard, everyone feared the disgusting odour of rotting straw — the smell of typhus. Simon knew that those who contracted the debilitating disease would be quarantined on arrival in the New World and would have to stay on an island near the port for as much as three weeks or however long the authorities deemed appropriate. Conditions were deplorable. Many in quarantine didn't make it out alive.

In the end, the brothers Simon and Sam were lucky enough to avoid the disease and weren't quarantined. Finally, they arrived in Boston's harbour and set foot in the New World.

Number one priority for these *grine kuzine*, green cousins or greenhorns, was to learn English so they could find work. It must have been a heady time for young men on their own in the world. Boston's city streets were filled with peddlers, dozens of languages in the air, food

Part 5

aplenty if you had the money, including some foodstuffs in weird metal cans, and so many novel sights and sounds that the heads of the newly arrived must have been sent spinning.

Like 60 percent of all Jewish immigrants at that time (according to an 1890 survey), Simon and Sam entered the "needle trades." The brothers trained to be tailors in Boston, where Simon lived for about four years. They were determined to avoid becoming shoemakers, a last-ditch occupation for Jewish immigrants who were unskilled at anything else. In addition to tailors, dressmakers, and hatters, Jewish immigrants in Boston worked as peddlers, clerks, painters, butchers, bakers, woodworkers, locksmiths, watch and clockmakers, cigar rollers, furriers, jewellers, bookbinders, and musicians. A nephew of Simon's became a small manufacturer of eyeglass lenses. Some Jewish immigrants also worked as glaziers, the occupation of my father's mother's family (Simon's second wife, Elizabeth), German immigrants in Cleveland who glazed many of the stained-glass windows in churches on Cleveland's West Side.

Boston was once known as "the New Jerusalem," and from 1875 to 1925 it certainly was that for the 50,000 to 70,000 Jewish immigrants who arrived there. Most Jews lived in the North and West Ends, the tenement districts, and many Jewish merchants opened stores along Salem Street. Simon likely joined one of the recreational, educational, or business clubs (*landsmanschaftn*), such as Hecht House, that were popular among Jews at the time, and perhaps studied English at evening classes there.

Bostonians would have reminded Simon that he was different, an outsider, and it's likely that he did everything in his power, like any immigrant, to fit in. A year or so later Simon would be standing at the rail of a ferry, looking dapper in his well-tailored clothes. Another well-dressed young fellow would strike up a conversation. When Simon replied, the fellow recoiled in shock and disgust on hearing Simon's accent. Simon was embarrassed and remembered this incident for the rest of his life, always working hard to eliminate his accent.

Boston was a particularly elitist city, hostile to both Jews and Catholics, whether Irish or Italian. In 1891 the *Boston Register* declared, metaphorical nose in the air, that there were only 8,000 "proper Bostonians." All were men and almost all were Protestant except for a handful of Catholics.

One Jew made the list: Louis Brandeis, a brilliant liberal lawyer who was eventually appointed to the U.S. Supreme Court. This despite the fact that the first known Jew in the United States, Solomon Franco, a scholar and trader, arrived in Boston as early as 1649.

Simon eventually left Boston for Cleveland, sometime around 1900. At that time Cleveland's garment industry was second only to New York City's in the United States. The Jewish community was burgeoning and numbered 90,000 by the 1920s. Interestingly enough, Simon didn't join the main Jewish population on the East Side of Cleveland but moved to the near West Side. Not feeling a strong religious connection to the Jewish faith, he was likely trying to pull away from the Jewish community and establish himself as a citizen remade in the American mould.

Less than ten years after arriving in Cleveland, Simon had a wife and three young children and had established a successful tailor's shop.

Then the building collapsed.

Part 6

1
Black Sheep

In my family I feel that I was always looked upon as the black sheep (or, in geologic terms, the "erratic"), and moving to the wilds of Quebec only cemented that attitude into place. I was on the phone with my mother — the pay phone nearest to the Farm, about six miles away.

"Of course, we want to come visit, dear. We want to see where you live."

"Well, I don't know. It's pretty rough."

"Oh, don't be silly. Don't you remember all those summers we took you kids up to my cousin's cottage on Georgian Bay? I *have* used an outhouse, you know."

"I just want to warn you. Don't expect too much. It's pretty wild country, and there's no electricity or running water in the cabin. And there's no motel nearby."

"There was no electricity at the cottage, either. Don't you remember, dear? We made do."

"I'm not really trying to talk you out of it — I just want you to be prepared."

My mother had always had a way with words — or at least with sayings. She was legendary in the family for coming up with old, forgotten sayings that she had heard in her youth. "There's no such thing as a five-minute job" was one of her favourites. When I tended to tasks and repairs around the cabin and farm, that saying became a constant refrain, as tasks consistently proved more difficult and time-consuming than anticipated.

In an old dwelling such as mine, there was never a lack of things to mend, repair, adjust, replace, or tear out. I might hope to make a quick job of one of these, such as replacing a cracked pane of glass in a window, for example, so I could get on to the next dozen jobs that clamoured for my attention. As I worked on the cracked pane, I would realize that the putty had fallen out from parts of three other panes and that the little piece of glass that was left over from the previous job was wide enough but not high enough and a trip to a neighbour's or a distant store was required. As one simple task blossomed into six or eight or ten others, I would hear those words: "There is no such thing as a five-minute job."

Another favourite saying of my mother's was: "Not all the bandits live in Mexico." She employed this slogan whenever she felt the price of an item was too high. This was true of almost everything, since her economic reality was firmly entrenched in Depression-era prices. She was never quite able to understand that the exchange rate between the U.S. and Canadian dollars meant that the prices on Canadian goods were not to be compared literally with the prices on U.S. goods. "Oh, my God! Canadian women should boycott this store!" she'd say, nearly fainting at the prices of canned goods or fruit or vegetables in Canadian stores. Finally, I resorted to going through my kitchen cupboards and removing the price stickers on all my canned and packaged foods before an impending visit.

I never discovered the source of another of her occasional sayings: "A stiff prick has no conscience." Not a subject to discuss with one's mother.

Three weeks after the phone call, my parents pulled their long Buick convertible into the grassy entranceway of the Farm. It was the end of August. There was no way they could have been prepared for what met them. My parents weren't campers — had never camped out in their lives. Yes, they had some experience of cottage life, but this was different.

It had been a long, mid-continental summer of high heat and even higher humidity. The grass in the field in front of the cabin was chest-high. The bush felt like a rainforest, with lots of soaking electrical storms and weeks of strong sun forcing the greenery to blaze out of control. The perfect germinating weather for all sorts of bugs, including fleas.

Part 6

My parents' arrival coincided with the first and only flea outbreak we ever had at the cabin. What with a house full of cats as carriers, by the end of a scorching August the fleas had taken over. Steve and Shirley were sleeping in their teepee, Paul and Colleen were staying a stone's throw away in their large surveyor's tent, and Jochen and I were sleeping outside on nights when there was no rain. We resorted to the necessary chemicals to rid ourselves of the pests but soon discovered that we had swept up the white powder too soon, not realizing the eggs would germinate again. When my parents arrived, the fleas were out of control.

After driving up from Cleveland by way of Toronto, Anabel and Rennie stumbled across the field on the well-worn path, my mother carrying an iron pot filled with spaghetti sauce and meatballs that she had hauled all the way in the trunk of the car, the pot lid taped on to avoid spillage. She had lied to the customs inspectors when asked if she was bringing anything into Canada. "Oh, no," she had said, "nothing, nothing at all."

Meanwhile, the trunk was bursting with box upon box of foodstuffs that she was smuggling into a land that obviously lacked such basics as Oreo cookies, onion-flavoured crackers, Licorice Allsorts, and tins of tuna fish. My mother never arrived anywhere without tins of tuna fish, which she would find at bargain prices "too good to leave on the shelf." There was also vodka poured into empty plastic shampoo bottles, bourbon in empty ginger ale bottles, and enough red wine to keep an army of Italian bricklayers happy for a month. As we crossed the field, my father and I struggled with several of these boxes, while my mother chattered on. "There's two large cans of pork and beans for lunch tomorrow, and I brought some bacon for breakfast, and, oh, my God, Rennie, did you check on the roast of pork to make sure it's still cool?" Then, turning to me, she said, "You do have an oven, don't you?"

"Yes, of course, but, Mom, pork roast in this heat?"

"Well, it'll go bad if we don't cook it. You don't have a fridge, right?"

We stopped to rest at the bottom of the little hill and faced the cabin before us. They inspected it for a moment.

"It looks sturdy enough," my dad commented.

"Keeps the rain off your head?" my mother asked.

I nodded.

She paused, looking around at the tree-covered hills. "Are there … bears?"

"Sometimes. But bears aren't the problem at the moment."

"Oh? What do you mean, dear?"

"We've got a flea outbreak."

"Fleas? Oh, my. That doesn't sound good."

"Why don't you poison 'em?" my dad suggested.

"Well, we did, but I guess we swept the powder up too soon — we didn't want the cats to eat it — and now the fleas are back. Anyway, no one can sleep in the house because it's infested. Sorry." I felt terrible. My parents, although not ancient, certainly weren't young.

"We'll have to sleep in the car." My father glanced back up the path to the road where his long lean Buick convertible was parked.

"Oh, my," said my mother.

―――――

We were still taking meals inside the cabin despite the fleas, and everyone gathered that evening for a feast of pork roast, one of my mother's specialties. The wood stove was booming and smoking (my first wood stove had numerous cracks in it), heating up the downstairs of the cabin on this muggy August evening. I was running around, trying to make sure my parents were as comfortable as possible in the circumstances, lighting lamps, cooking, introducing Steve, Shirley, Jochen, Paul, and Colleen to the folks, pouring wine and generally being as convivial as possible. This was their first visit to my first house, and I wanted it to go well.

My mother spent an hour pulling packages and cans out of boxes and bags or ordering my father to find this or that as she stocked the shelves in the cupboards until they groaned under the unaccustomed weight. Meanwhile, I was cooking potatoes and vegetables for the roast, sweating over the wood stove, and swigging wine with abandon.

Finally, dinner was ready and everyone sat down at the rough kitchen table, decorated with homemade carvings of leaves and flowers randomly dug into its wooden surface. Everyone was enjoying the food, the wine, and the talk, when I leaped up from the table, yanked down my trousers without thinking, caught a flea on my thigh, and disposed of it. Then Steve did the same. My parents looked a little stunned, and my mother became unusually quiet.

"Sorry," I said, bowing over my plate, "but the little buggers drive ya nuts."

My mother raised her feet to the first rung of her chair.

Later, taking a flashlight, I walked my dad out to the car. My mother decided to stay behind for a while in the kitchen, talking and drinking vodka with the "young people." After I went up to bed (it was raining lightly, so I had to brave the fleas inside) and everyone else was gone, I could hear her crying softly with a commiserating Steve.

"No, really, he's all right." Steve was referring to me. "He loves it here."

"But it's so rough. The damn stove smokes. There's fleas ... there's ..." She wept softly, whimpering.

"No, really, it's all right. It's not so bad. We all like it here." A moment of silence. "Another drink, Mrs. Frutkin? Sorry there's no ice cubes."

"Yes, please, dear." The sound of a glass sliding across the table. "I didn't want him to go to the war, but this ..." I imagined her looking about the smoke-stained cabin. "Oh, God ..."

My parents never complained to me, even though the night was hot and sticky and a little rainy, so they must have had to sleep in the hot car with the windows rolled up. I asked my dad how his night was in the Buick and he said, "A little tight. Not so bad." But I noticed he walked crookedly the first hour.

That morning my parents drove to the village of Wakefield and found a motel to stay in for the rest of their three-day visit.

Eventually, we bought more powder to kill the fleas and left it out until the cold weather arrived. The cats knew to stay away from it and didn't get sick, and my parents returned to Cleveland assured that I remained the black sheep of the family.

I had enough canned tuna to last six months.

2
Orzo

FAMILY VISITS WERE ALWAYS fraught with tension. The first visit to the cabin by my brother, Larry, his wife, Dolores, and their two young girls occurred a few years later. I was already living with my first wife, Janet. Of course, we wanted to make a good impression on my brother and his family who were driving all the way up from the United States and staying at a hotel in Ottawa.

Janet and I decided that we would make a special dinner, using orzo, an Italian pasta that looks like rice. We had never worked with it before, and though we both had significant experience cooking on the wood stove, we knew there were times that, no matter how hard one tried, the stove, the fire, and the heat were too difficult to control to allow for an altogether successful meal.

Larry was a lawyer and something of a gourmand, and enjoyed travelling and eating in France and England, and Dolores was a fine cook who had served us many excellent meals at their home in Indianapolis during visits there, so this provided added pressure for the "dinner." They were definitely not vegetarians or back-to-the-land types.

The day of the visit arrived in early autumn. My brother pulled up with his little family in tow. I went out to the car to meet them as they loaded their youngest into a stroller and took their oldest girl by the hand. We all trudged along the path across the field toward the cabin, the stroller bumping over the rough terrain.

My brother seemed hesitant but, good spirit that he was, he didn't say anything.

We entered the cabin. They had arrived in late afternoon, and by the time everyone was settled in the kitchen, it was already getting dark. I went into my usual panic, running around trying to light the coal-oil lamps (and refilling them, as they always ran out at inconvenient times), keeping the fire in the stove going so we could cook, and trying to make everyone comfortable.

For people who spend most of their lives in the electrified and convenient suburbs, the cabin was always a bit of a shock. The kitchen, with its single window whose light was effectively blocked by a bush growing outside it, always descended into dusk long before the surrounding fields. The three oil lamps in the kitchen lit portions of the room but threw other parts into deep shadow. The rest of the house, including the sitting room next to the kitchen, was completely dark because it was too dangerous (and not economical) to have lamps or candles lit in unattended rooms. This must have seemed rather strange for the two little girls, as well as for my brother and his wife. The discovery that there was no indoor bathroom and one had to carry a lamp to the outhouse caused further consternation. No one complained. But I could see the worried looks on their faces.

Meanwhile, Janet was cooking up the tomato vegetable concoction we were going to serve over the orzo, which was my responsibility. In order to get the water boiling sufficiently to cook the pasta, I had to stoke the fire, and the kitchen turned into a sweatbox. Once I dumped the pasta in, I couldn't moderate the heat in the stove. I was so busy with lamps and drinks and trying to keep everyone happy and comfortable that I let the orzo overcook. Badly. The dinner was a disaster, the orzo resembling thick paste. No one complained, but the rice-like pasta looked a little like mashed maggots.

Our visitors gagged their meal down, grabbed up the little girls, and immediately fled for the safety of their hotel in Ottawa. Ten minutes after they left I noticed they had forgotten the baby stroller. I rushed out with it, hopped in my car (I had one by that time), and sped off, hoping to intercept them. I finally did catch up sixty minutes later — in the parking lot of their hotel in the West End of Ottawa. My brother was just getting their bags out of the trunk and glanced up, giving me a decidedly confused look.

I handed him the stroller. "You forgot this."

A little stunned, he said, "Oh, thanks. You drove all the way down with it?"

"Yeah, I thought I could catch you, but I couldn't. I thought you might need it." I indicated the stroller.

"Oh." I could see him thinking, *What's the big deal? It's just a cheap stroller. I can easily buy another one.*

"Yeah. So ... good to see you." I turned and left.

I felt there was more than a simple stroller involved, but neither of us could say anything. We had a hard time communicating in those days, my brother and I. He couldn't see the sense of my world, and I had, at the time, rejected parts of his. I wanted to say something like: "Sorry for the rotten meal. Sorry the cabin is so funky and uncomfortable. Sorry you couldn't have enjoyed the visit more. Sorry we have trouble connecting." Neither of us knew what to say, so we said nothing.

3
Endocarditis

LIBRARY AND ARCHIVES CANADA records that there were four Drouins killed in the First World War and one Drouin killed in the Second World War, none from the villages of Wolf Lake or the Mashams. The Archives lists a total of ninety Drouins in the Canadian military in the First World War, including one Louis Drouin, and a Philibert Drouin, who was court-martialled in 1917 for "conduct to the prejudice of good order and military discipline."

Recruits for the First World War were required to fill out Attestation Papers for the Canadian Expeditionary Force in which they answered twelve questions such as the following: What is your name? In what Town, Township, or Parish, and in what Country were you born? What is your trade or calling? Are you willing to be vaccinated or revaccinated?

Considering that almost all the Drouins listed lived in Quebec and were almost certainly French-speaking, a surprisingly small percentage of the forms were in French. Almost all were in English, although the

Part 6

answers written by recruits were in English, in French, or in an odd combination of the two. For example, one recruit wrote "single" in answer to the question "Are you married?" and filled in "Fromager" (cheesemaker) under "Trade or Calling."

The overleaf of the Attestation Paper was to be filled in with the physical description of the recruit and included a box for "Distinctive marks and genital peculiarities." Why they were interested in genital peculiarities, I don't know, unless it was an attempt to determine who was circumcised. Also included was a section on Religious Denominations. The applicant was to choose one of the following (they were presented in this order): Church of England, Presbyterian, Methodist, Baptist or Congregationalist, Other Protestants, Roman Catholic, Jewish. This list alone is indicative of a certain pecking order endemic to the Canadian society of the day.

The first names among the Drouins listed are an intriguing lot that covers the range from Greek and Roman influences to the biblical: Cenaphile, Fortunat, Eusebe, Gaudias, Heliodore, Salomon, Tancrede, Theodule, Urgel, Hormidas. The last was a young single recruit from Ste-Cécile-de-Masham who was listed as a farmer. How strange that I can discover he was five feet four inches and had a dark complexion, black hair, and blue eyes, but can also learn such intimacies as the scars he carried on his knees and right calf as well as his lingering endocarditis, an enlargement of the heart lining, often the result of rheumatic fever. The presence of endocarditis, however, wasn't enough to keep him out of the 2nd Depot Battalion, Eastern Ontario Regiment, the stamp that appears at the top of his papers.

Like Hormidas, many of the other Drouin recruits listed themselves as farmers. Along with lumbermen, farmers were the most common category of trade or calling (*calling* — such a fascinating, archaic term), with the odd butter-maker, cheese-maker, mechanic, and clerk signing up. Needless to say, all were young, most between the ages of eighteen and twenty-three. It is clear from this selection that the great majority of recruits came from poor, mostly rural, families.

The term *poverty draft* is used to describe the Vietnam-era draft when students in college or university were given automatic deferments to allow them to continue their education while those who couldn't afford university were drafted. It has been common throughout history that draftees could buy themselves out of service if they had the money, as was the case in the American Civil War. The U.S. military during the Vietnam War, and still today, consists overwhelmingly of sons (and now daughters) of the poor, both black and white. The U.S. military today shamelessly advertises life in the army as an adventure, more thrilling than a video game, or a ticket to college or a good job.

The typical eighteen-year-old has no idea what he wants to do with his life, is focused for the most part on getting away from his parents, and considers himself immortal. Ripe pickings for recruiters. In recognition of the vast untapped potential of younger recruits, the U.S. military has Junior ROTC (Reserve Officer Training Corps) programs in over 3,200 high schools in the United States (2006), where the virtues of war are extolled and few of its dangers mentioned. The Pentagon spends over $2.5 billion per year on recruiting (Source: American Friends Service Committee), with inflated promises of job training and flashy TV advertisements that make basic training, and life in the military in general, look like a rock video. Military recruitment in the United States is now a smart bomb, with perfect focus on its selected target.

4
Vietnem Vet

DURING THE VIETNAM ERA, desperate recruiters didn't bother weeding out recruits like Jim, one of the friends who travelled in the bread truck with me when I first moved to Canada and was with me when I found the Farm. I always picture him behind the wheel of one of two vehicles: a military jeep or our bread truck/camper. A recent veteran of Vietnam, Jim was an old friend of Wally, my farm co-purchaser from Dover, Ohio. Jim was a natural-born grifter who could use his charm to beat the system and use the military for his own ends.

Part 6

Recently, Jim had returned to the small central Ohio town of Dover after a year in the Vietnam War, working in radio repair and medical evacuation details. His military tour was finished, but it was hard for him to leave behind what he had experienced there. Wally, Jim, and I would hang out in a cramped, chilly room, an old root cellar, in the basement of Jim's family home (this was the spring of 1970, while I was teaching elementary school in the suburbs of Cleveland and before I was drafted).

Jim was a quintessential American guy — six foot one, blond, lean, good-looking. He liked to say he hid out in this basement room because he was afflicted with bad hay fever, but it wasn't hay fever season. Perhaps he was hiding out from the demons that still haunted him from halfway around the world. The stories of his horrific experiences in Vietnam poured out of him. Wally and I willingly shared the job of audience, therapist, shrink.

In Vietnam, Jim had held a wide variety of jobs and seemed to move constantly from one posting to another. His stories of working on medical evacuation were riveting and hair-raising, confirming our worst fears about the war. At the end of each day that he spent evacuating dead and wounded soldiers who had been caught in battle, he would have to throw away his uniform because it was so soaked in blood and gore. Everything I had read and heard about the Vietnam War came alive in his first-person accounts. Vietnam was no longer something I watched only on the daily news, a flickering image on the screen or a black-and-white photo in a newspaper. Here was a person who had been there and seen the worst.

Jim was also an endless schemer and scam artist. Outgoing and friendly, with a wacky sense of humour, he was one of those rare people who could talk their way around anything. Many of his schemes never saw the light of day, but once in a while, when someone came up with the money, a few of his crazy ideas actually bore fruit.

Maybe it was the clean white shirts he always wore that made people trust him — always a long-sleeved white shirt, unstarched but not wrinkled, the sleeves rolled up. The combination of pure white cloth and rolled-up sleeves seemed to say both "classy" and "down to earth." In any case, it always worked — people trusted him without hesitation.

Erratic North

After he arrived in Vietnam, it didn't take him long to form his own opinions about the war. He devoted much of his time and energy drumming up ways to sabotage the war effort in any way he could. Eventually, he managed to commandeer a jeep (somehow he had convinced those in charge that he was supposed to deliver it up-country to a colonel in some detachment or other) and used it for two months while he "got lost" and took a tour/vacation around the country, smoking some of the world's most powerful and effective pot, visiting Buddhist monasteries, getting to know the locals, and basically avoiding the war. It sounded like something straight out of Joseph Heller's *Catch-22*, albeit in a different time and place.

When he heard I wanted to go to Canada, Jim said he would come along for the ride and talked me into footing the bill for an old bread truck that had been converted into a camper with three beds. (He would pay me back later, he said. I'm still waiting, of course.) After I finished my year of teaching elementary school in Berea, Ohio, in 1969–70, Jim and I headed north. We were joined on the journey by Tim, another Dover resident, a quiet, gentle craftsman, who was the brother of a girl I was dating. Jim wasn't really interested in buying into the Farm because he wasn't a settler — he was definitely more the drifter type, more range rider than rancher.

After we reached the border at Buffalo, we crossed over the Peace Bridge and were promptly refused entry into Canada. I suppose we looked too ragged and scruffy and didn't have a good enough story to convince the border guards. I wasn't devastated, but I was definitely worried. If I couldn't even get into the country, what would I do then? At that time I hadn't been drafted yet, so the situation wasn't critical, but I could feel it coming. I wasn't ready yet to attempt swimming across the Niagara River. After talking it over, we decided to try another, smaller border crossing the next day. We headed across New York State and parked by the side of the highway, trucks passing all night as we slept in our sturdy camper. The next morning we pulled up to a small crossing with a single agent working in the booth that stood on Canadian soil.

He was young, and gave us a toothy smile. "Hi. Have any firearms?"

We looked at one another and shook our heads. Jim, who was driving, smiled and leaned out the window. "Nope. Don't like guns."

"Okay. Welcome to Canada."

We drove down the highway, ebullient, as well as relieved. We were in.

5
Bear

I **WATCHED AS A** stranger approached along the path toward the cabin. He was carrying a rifle loosely in his right hand.

"*Bonjour.* Me, I'm Gaston. You know Albert, down the road?" The stranger pointed. "He tell me you live here now."

"That's true. I'm Mark." We shook hands as Shirley and Steve raised their heads from the garden next to the cabin where they were on their knees pulling weeds. "Wanna beer?"

He nodded, and I went down to the spring box where we kept the beer cooling. Moments later the four of us gathered with our stubby bottles and sat in the afternoon sunlight on the ground-level seats around the firepit. Medium height with a slim build, Gaston had the rough look of a local — a small moustache, sandy brown hair, sleeveless white T-shirt, not particularly clean. He appeared to be about forty years old. His most distinguishing feature was a wide scar that ran from near his right shoulder down the side of his right arm to just below the elbow.

"I hunt bear, me. The bear come down here." He indicated a patch of ground on a small slope that ran behind the garden and disappeared into the bush. "Seen plenty here. They come for apple." We glanced at the two apple trees in the yard — one behind the garden, the other directly behind the house. The apples were starting to turn red. "Me, I shoot plenty of bear here, this spot."

"That thing loaded?" Steve asked.

"Sure. Never know. Don' wanna walk into damn bear on da road."

I could tell Steve didn't like him. "Well, you won't be doing any hunting around here now." This comment from Steve was met by an uncomfortable silence all around.

Shirley spoke up to relieve the tension. "That's quite the scar."

He nodded.

"From a bear?" I asked.

He nodded deeply. "*Oui*. A few winter ago, my brother bet me a case a beer, I not go into bear cave." He looked up and pointed. "On that mountain there. I go, me. Man, that cave stink. I go in, quiet, poke bear with stick, but bear not full asleep yet. Bear take swing at me, tear me arm. I get outta there fast. Zoom."

Shirley said, "I can see why you might want to carry the rifle after that."

"*Oui*."

A silent pause filled the air.

"You see any bear this place?" Gaston asked.

"No, not so far." I glanced at Steve and Shirley for confirmation.

"You see bear, you want I come and shoot?"

"No, I don't think so," I said. "We just don't want any hunting here, and so far the bears haven't been a problem."

Steve spoke up. "I think I saw some bear scat earlier today under that apple tree."

We all stood up, walked over, and stared at what appeared to be a small cow-pie. "Yep, bear," said Gaston. "Come eat apple."

"Well, that's okay," I ventured, trying to explain our position. "There's enough apples, anyway, so the bears can have a few."

Steve went back to the garden to work, Shirley joined him a moment later, and Gaston went on his way, his rifle over his shoulder.

It was clear we were sharing the Farm, this land, and these forests, with a number of other residents, beasts of all sorts, but bears had a way of making their presence known more than other creatures. Living up to thirty-two years, the black bear (*Ursus americanus*) can grow into a 600-pound behemoth, measuring six feet from head to tail. As of 2007, it is estimated that Ontario and Quebec have black bear populations of around 100,000 each, far more than any U.S. state except Alaska. North Carolina has about 11,000 and Pennsylvania approximately 15,000, for example. Their numbers appear to be growing, except in those regions where their habitat is disappearing. The black bear population in all of North America is now estimated to be approximately 800,000.

A week after meeting Gaston, Steve and I saw a bear walking above the stream at the far end of the Farm, at a spot where a waterfall tumbles from a high swamp and passes through a gorge. The bear was several hundred feet away, on the far side of the stream and separated from us by a steep cliff, so we felt fairly safe as we watched the black bear poking about in the bushes above the stream.

Another time I was out wandering alone in the autumn woods in an area at the foot of the mountain behind the cabin when I came across an adult black bear. I had just finished relieving my bowels in the forest and hadn't pulled up my pants yet when the bear rumbled by not ten feet away, looking extraordinarily light on his feet for his size. I don't believe he saw me, at least he gave no indication that he had, but I spotted him through a break in the brush and trees as he bounded past. My reaction was immediate and purely instinctual. Despite everything I had read and heard about the various ways to react to the presence of a bear, the only thought in my mind was *"Run!"* which I did, swiftly and in the opposite direction. I flew over rocky hillocks and through the woods, out into the field, across the stream, and down the road. I didn't stop until I was halfway home. As I panted, I listened and was sure the bear hadn't followed. I knew that a bear could easily outrun a man, especially through thick bush, but there was no way I was going to stick around to test that thesis.

The apple trees continued to draw bears down from the hills in the late summer and early autumn. The bears sometimes broke branches off in their desire to reach the most luscious fruit. Then Paul decided he wanted to try keeping bees and set up a few beehives along the edge of our front field. These, too, brought the bears out, apparently not for the honey as much as for the young bee larvae. After a hive was ripped apart, we spent the next several nights, noisemakers in hand, sitting out in the field hidden behind some brush waiting for the bears to return, hoping to protect the other three hives. Dave had constructed a wooden clapper that looked like two very large hands, which was supposed to be a wondrously effective bear scarer. Paul even borrowed a rifle for one evening, but never spotted anything to shoot at. Somehow we managed to keep the bears away long enough so Paul could bring his honey in.

Honey and apples sounds like a fairly pleasant diet. I had to question the bears' culinary discernment, however, when, the next summer, Paul placed a garbage bag full of dirty disposable diapers (from his and Colleen's infant, Oona) on the roof of the little cabin he had built about a hundred yards from my place. Placing the garbage up high was a vain attempt to keep it away from porcupines and raccoons. But the unexpected happened. A bear went up on the low-angled roof, ripped the garbage bag open, and licked the diapers clean.

For years I had vivid dreams about bears entering the cabin while I was asleep. Although it never happened, I was convinced there was no stopping a hungry bear from entering once it had decided there was food to be had behind those wooden walls. In fact, a bear had once reached through the screen in the kitchen window of my cabin in order to help himself to a compost bucket filled with vegetable scraps that sat just under the window.

A locked wooden door is nothing to a bear — a single blast from a bear's paw can split a door down the middle or tear if off its hinges. The power of a bear is extraordinary and merits great respect. Black bears are mostly vegetarian but not entirely, and hunger can drive a bear to act abnormally. Also, bears have been known to develop a taste for meat.

When I first moved to the Farm, I shared the cabin with a gentler animal — a groundhog. He had "the basement apartment," which he approached through a hole he had dug just to the right of my front-door entrance. The cabin had a three-foot-high dirt cellar underneath, which I never used, so the groundhog stayed on for a while. I recall one day standing inside the house looking out my front window as the groundhog made his way back home. After a day of wandering, he approached the cabin from the field in front. He stopped every several steps, pulled a yellow buttercup over to mouth level with his paw, and bit off the flower. He was in absolutely no hurry and appeared to be living an idyllic existence.

Part 6

The cabin attracted snakes, too, in profusion. Garter snakes loved to bask on the stones in the sun in front of the cabin or rest in any place on the south-facing wall where they could find enough purchase, usually on a space where the cement chinking between the squared logs left sufficient room. Years later, when my son was about five, a snake that had been sunbathing on a log directly above the front door partly lost his footing (if snakes can be said to lose their "footing") and dropped suddenly into the open doorway, dangling right in front of us. A woman friend visiting from the city let out a piercing shriek, and the snake fell and slithered away. From that day on my son developed a severe snake phobia and religiously avoided tall grass. After I left the Farm, another friend spent a weekend there to do a meditation retreat and was constantly bothered by the arrival of garter snakes inside the cabin.

Wasps with their nests in the walls often found their way inside, as well, and I was bitten more than once, having sat down unknowingly on a chair or couch where a wasp was already resting; mice scurried all night in the attic; bats in the bedrooms occasionally had to be trapped in a colander and released outside; ants and moths and mosquitoes — the cabin was home to innumerable beasts.

Despite the fact that the nearest village to the Farm was called Wolf Lake, I heard wolves only once in my ten years at the Farm. It was late at night in the dead of winter. I was alone in the cabin. Suddenly, out of the silence, the unmistakable howl came from a nearby hill. Never before had I experienced what is meant by the expression "the hair stood up on the back of my head." And then an answering howl came from another hill. And another howl from another direction. And so on for the next two hours. I was able to count six or seven wolves. It was riveting and primal.

I suspect that fear of wolves and snakes is still deeply ingrained in the human psyche. It's an instinctive survival mechanism that one takes precautions on hearing the sound of a wolf's howl. I marvelled that it was still possible to hear the cry of wolves in the 1970s, a mere one-hour drive from the capital of Canada. A day later news spread that a pack of wolves (*a pack of wolves* — it had a positively medieval sound to it) had come down from up north in a season of low food supply.

In order to visit friends who lived on other parts of the Farm in the evening, I had to walk the empty, pitch-black road to return home later at night. The road back home passed by a swamp where the dark was impenetrable and eerie. I had no desire to see a pair of red eyes, glowing like hot marmalade — or worse, a half-dozen pairs — staring at me from out of that swamp. I didn't do much visiting for the next month.

6
Wood Thrush

I LOOKED FORWARD TO that moment in the early spring when I would notice a subtle change in the wind — no longer sounding hard and empty as it passed through bare branches but rich and abundant as it washed through fresh new leaves. The world suddenly seemed a softer place as the wind — now it could be called a breeze — soughed through the lush tapestry of watery green on the surrounding hills. I felt my body begin to relax with the warm, soft air of spring, the tension of winter leaving my muscles, my blood, the earth itself. It was a sound I welcomed like an old friend returning from a long journey, like those trailing wedges of Canada geese honking high in a blue sky, heading north.

Because the Farm was normally such a quiet place, sounds tended to stand out with great clarity. Late spring was the noisiest season. From first light until late at night the world was singing. A chorus of birds, literally thousands of birds of all descriptions, greeted the nacreous light of dawn, beginning their melodies, territory marking, and mating calls long before the sun made its appearance. The cacophony of chirps and trills was so intense and extravagant outside my open window on the second floor of the cabin that I could never sleep past 5:30 a.m. in May or June. Eventually, the chorus tailed off into the sounds that punctuate a normal spring day.

Part 6

In the evening, if I happened to be walking along the road, I might pass a pool or a flooded area along a stream where the profuse, bird-like noise of the frogs, the "spring peepers," was so loud and piercing it made my ears ache. In ancient Egypt, frogs were considered the heralds of fertility because they appeared in the Nile several days before it flooded the surrounding fields, ensuring a deposit of rich silt and the abundance of the next season's crops. And, fittingly, Jochen's garden, situated in the flood plain of the stream, boasted the richest soil on the Farm.

Also at evening time, in the resinous light of dusk, the gorgeous song of the wood thrush could be heard echoing out of the darkening forest. There was always one on the hillside nearest my cabin, its bubbling, trilling, flute-like knock a rich aural feast to end the day.

Later, sitting in the kitchen of the cabin, reading before a coal-oil lamp as night settled in, I would hear thousands of insects, mosquitoes in particular, whining at the screen doors and windows, as well as the occasional interloper that had found its way inside.

At any time of year it was intriguing to notice how easily and how far the human voice travelled among these enclosing hills. I could hear my neighbours talking in a normal voice a quarter of a mile away, and if someone laughed or shouted, the audible distance could easily double. The bark of a dog and the hollow knock of woodpeckers, as well, journeyed great distances through the green silence.

Winter, without a doubt, was the quietest season, the silences as deep as the black spaces between stars. In fact, the silence had a special quality in this place and each silence had its own subtle character. There was the silence of thick flakes of snow falling in slow motion, the silence of the first ray of winter sun breaking the horizon, the silence of a grey jay standing perfectly still on the branch of an alder bush. It was startling to hear, as I sat reading late on a frozen January night, a cedar in the swamp let off a crack like a shot from a rifle.

Whatever the season, I was particularly fond of birds that called their own name, especially the whippoorwill, whose call echoes out of the deep forest on warm summer nights. A member of the nightjar family, whippoorwills are also known as goatsuckers, owing to an ancient superstition that these birds blinded goats by sucking milk from their udders. How in the world the bird got this reputation is anyone's guess. I wonder, was there a big problem with blind goats in antiquity?

Only once did I actually sight a whippoorwill. I was in the yard between the cabin and the garden. It was almost dark, and a good-size bird (it appeared slightly larger than a blue jay) landed on one of the garden's fence posts. It was too dark to make out its colouring or precise shape, but then I heard a slight knocking or clicking in the bird's throat followed by its signature call: "Whip-poor-will! Whip-poor-will! Whip-poor-will!" Never again would one come so close; in fact, they seemed to instinctively keep their distance, so I counted myself lucky to have seen one at all.

Another bird that calls its own name is the friendly black-capped chickadee, a half-dozen of the little grey, white, and black birds a happy sight on a winter day, tumbling about in a hazelnut bush next to the cabin, calling (also in threes): "Chick-a-dee-dee-dee." And, of course, the little phoebe cries "Phoebe, phoebe" (in twos, generally) all the long summer day as he seeks a mate.

The loudmouths of the forest are the crows, complaining from their high branches or uttering their guttural squawks as they sweep low in the valley. According to French-Canadian legends, as related by Edith Fowke in *Folktales of French Canada*, the crow received its coarse voice and its black feathers as a curse from Noah. Noah had asked the crow to go forth from the Ark during the Great Flood, look for green trees, and return with a branch. But the crow saw dead bodies floating on the water and decided to "satisfy his voracious appetite," having itself a feast and forgetting its duty. For this the crow was punished with an unpleasant voice. Blue jays, too, are considered noisome birds. Their sharp warning cry in the cedar forest behind the cabin always sparked something of a sense of melancholy in me, perhaps because they appear more prevalent in fall and signal the end of fine weather.

The sounds of certain birds are profoundly subtle and are often missed entirely or remain unrecognized by the casual visitor to the forest — the thumping of the partridge, for example. It seems to be felt in the chest rather than heard with the ears, as if one's lungs were reverberating slightly in responsive echo.

Part 6

A few birds seem to emanate a special silence. The marsh hawk circling high above in cloudless sky of immense clarity. The great blue heron standing in a pool along the stream, utterly still and silent, waits and waits as it stares at its own reflection. And, finally, the pileated woodpecker, which I sighted once only. Larger than a crow, with its red crest and long bill, it has a thoroughly primeval look, suggestive of a pterodactyl. It emanates an ancient silence as it soars soundlessly through a stand of high pines. Apparently, its primitive cry was traditionally employed for stock background noise in old jungle films.

The Farm and surrounding countryside were a veritable theatre of birds. Barn swallows swept split-tailed through the empty upper windows of a ruined log cabin. A young marsh hawk, an eyas covered in immature feathers, not yet able to fly, already displayed a tough disposition as it viciously attacked the stick I offered through the reeds where I stumbled upon it. Or a flock of snow buntings that literally "rolled" through a field of powder as the birds foraged, those in the rear flying to the front, over and over, so the flock looked as if it was tumbling in a wave across open winter fields.

And, lastly, I can recall the first time I heard a loon, with its indescribable, haunting warble, sounding like a madwoman lost in the woods. The strange sound must have terrified the first settlers and made them feel as if they had arrived in a place filled with the murmurs and howls of wandering ghosts. Perhaps it was this ghostly quality that convinced the Chippewa in their belief that it was the loon that created the world.

Part 7

I

Cemetery: Autumn 2004

During my visit earlier with Hazel, the former Wolf Lake post lady, I learned that Louis Drouin was buried in the nearby Wolf Lake cemetery. Some months later I invited an old friend, Murray, to come along on a journey to Wolf Lake to visit the cemetery where I hoped to find Louis's gravestone. On the day in question, I pulled into Murray's driveway and, due to a gammy hip, he stiff-legged his way into my Camry. As we drove up into the Gatineau Hills, I related the story of Louis and, as we neared Wolf Lake, I decided to stop and show Murray the abandoned field that had once been the site of Louis's farm.

I pulled into the empty green space just off the highway, no sign left of the farm or the test fire by the volunteer brigade that had levelled the farm buildings some twenty years before. The short-lived rain shower we had passed through earlier had blossomed into a clear sky, like a blue flower with a hot, late-summer sun as its corolla. We grunted out of the car, letting the sounds of the road dissipate in the hushed country silence.

Although Louis's farm was completely gone and invisible, there *were* ghosts of a farm that once had been. The fallen limb of a nearby tree resembled one of Louis's workhorses: the thick Manitoba maple branch, grey with time and weather, imitated with startling accuracy the appearance of a long-necked horse, the horse branch with its head stuck up into the leaves of the tree from whence it had tumbled. The location was uncanny — it was within feet of the place where Louis's workhorses had once long ago been stabled.

On the far side of the tree, we found more invisible presences: a patch of soft grass under a tree, flattened, likely by a sleeping bear or perhaps a family of deer. We also discovered a foot-long leaf of wasp-nest paper, looking like something that had fallen from the portfolio of a Japanese artist.

We drank from our plastic bottles of water in the now-scorching sun and decided to leave — the graveyard at Lac des Loups beckoned.

Driving to the far end of Wolf Lake, we passed houses with bright yellow Russian sunflowers standing tall outside their front doors. Before taking the turn at the crossroads for the graveyard, we decided to stop at the Wolf Lake church, a rather severe structure with a statue of St. Francis standing out front, seemingly bereft with no birds in his hands.

The church, built of concrete blocks, was perhaps the least decorative theological structure I have ever encountered. The single item of note was a stone above the entrance with the following letters carved in majuscule: ST-FRS-D'ASS. No waste of effort here. (I suppose someone with little knowledge of the Roman Catholic religion might think the church was called Saint Furs of Ass.) Underneath this less than effusive title, a few letters and numbers had been carved: W 1939 L.

Murray and I speculated that the *W* and the *L* stood for Wolf Lake, but that seemed rather odd since the priest had almost certainly been French-speaking and would have referred to the place as Lac des Loups. The only visitors on this late morning (in fact, the entire village appeared deserted) were several dozen wasps with dangling legs that floated before the sun-drenched church front, resembling tiny men in hang gliders. Perhaps they were lost souls who had once missed a Sunday Mass generations ago and were now trying to find a way in to seek forgiveness.

Leaving church and wasps behind, we headed over to the cemetery, less than a quarter of a mile away and behind the local elementary school. Through a latched metal fence we entered a cemetery of extreme simplicity. Clipped, patchy grass grew between the stone markers set in rows, a few weeds here and there. There were no gushing beds of flowers; no fresh flowers left on graves. At a distance the graveyard could have been mistaken for a hayfield. About four rows away I spotted a large gravestone constructed in the shape of two intersecting hearts with the name Drouin on it. From my vantage point it appeared that the grave had a leaping fish carved in its centre, but on closer inspection this turned out to be, disappointingly, a pair of praying hands and it was the wrong Drouin, in any case.

Murray and I wandered aimlessly for a while, checking names and

Part 7

dates. One grave must have belonged to a music lover or a musician, for it had a violin and bow carved on it. At the far edge of the cemetery we found four graves that consisted of simple wooden crosses of white, about a foot high, that had red crosses painted on them in a rather slapdash manner. No names. We wondered aloud.

"Unbaptized infants maybe?" Murray suggested. "Or perhaps they were criminals."

"Suicides?"

We noted that many of the gravestones had the names of entire families carved on them: father, mother, children. The *birth* dates of the family members were already etched into place, while blank spaces were left for the *death* dates of those who hadn't succumbed to their fates yet. The earliest date of a death we could find was 1888, but there was no sign of the grave of Louis Drouin.

Murray and I decided to take a more organized approach in our search for Louis and began to walk the rows systematically like the priest and his acolyte passing along pews with the collection basket. None of the dead coughed up any coins, but we did find a Wolf Lake graveyard memorial to woodcutters near the centre of the cemetery, completely overgrown with weeds and low bushes. It consisted of a wooden plaque mounted on a huge round iron saw with serrated edges. Several lumbermen's tools were affixed to the saw — an axe and a grappling iron with a long wooden handle. The plaque read: "In Memoriam — To Our Ancestors. Our heritage is their confidence in God and their faith in the future." (Translation from the original French by M. Wilson.)

Before heading for the gate, I decided to check one last row along the margin of the cemetery by the nearby woods. In the dark shadows thrown by pines and spruce, I found what I was looking for.

Murray came over, and we gazed at the marker:

    b. 1903 Louis Drouin   d. 1979
    Spouse of
    b. 1926 Maria Belisle   d. ____
    b. 1963 Alain Drouin   d. 1964
    b. 1966 Claudette Drouin d. 1966

Louis's spouse, who was twenty-three years younger than him, was still alive. I had had no idea that he and his wife had lost two infants in two years. He had never mentioned it.

We stood and stared for a few minutes, listened to the silence of afternoon and the wind high in the trees, a bird calling in the distance. We said nothing, and then decided to leave. Backing out of the cemetery, I swung the gate shut behind us and we drove home.

2
The Wall

THE VIETNAM VETERANS MEMORIAL Wall in Washington, D.C., is known simply as the Wall or "the wall that heals." It is a place of quiet memory and contemplation, a site of profound sadness. It speaks to people with its eloquent simplicity. Dedicated in 1982, the Wall is inscribed with the names of 58,245 U.S. military personnel killed or missing in action during the Vietnam War, from a total of 2.7 million who served. Vietnam was a man's world — only eight of the deceased listed on the Wall are women.

Jan Scruggs, the wounded Vietnam vet who instigated the establishment of a Vietnam memorial, was inspired by the film *The Deer Hunter*, with its realistic depiction of the war and how it affected soldiers who had served. Scruggs stated: "I think it will make people feel the price of war ... it will make them understand that the price has to be paid in human lives."

In 1980 a competition was held for a design of the monument. One of the four criteria required for design submissions had read: "Make no political statement about the war." The eight well-known architects and sculptors on the jury unanimously chose from 1,421 entries a design by a completely unknown Yale University architecture student, Maya Ying Lin, whose parents had fled China in 1949.

Part 7

Maya Lin, engaged in architectural studies at the Yale School of Architecture, brought to the discipline, from her own background, the traditional Chinese and Japanese spirit of balance and harmony. The Wall is constructed of two black slabs of granite from Bangalore, India, that stretch for about 246 feet each, one pointing at the Washington Monument and the other pointing at the Lincoln Memorial. From the air, the Wall resembles the pair of compasses held by the epic figure, often mistaken for Almighty God, in William Blake's famous etching *The Ancient of Days*.

The black granite used in the monument has a highly reflective, mirror-like surface. Because the viewer sees both a name and his or her own reflection, past and present are brought together.

The Wall stirred immediate controversy among veterans' groups, some of whom found the design too abstract and unpatriotic. In some complaints there was a racist suggestion that the memorial shouldn't be designed by an oriental. For this reason Maya Ying Lin's name wasn't mentioned at the dedication. Ultimately, most veterans, their families, and other Americans have come not only to accept the Wall but also to admire it. An astonishing 3.7 million people visited the memorial in 2005.

Of those listed on the Wall, 997 were killed on their first day in Vietnam and 1,448 were killed on the last day of their tour of duty. Cruel numbers. The monument is indeed a kind of mirror: Twenty-nine soldiers listed have the same birth date as me, and thirty-five are from Parma, Ohio, where I was raised. There are twelve names mistakenly etched on the wall that belong to men who were still alive at the time of its unveiling.

What was really involved for the soldiers is brought home when one reads the causes of death listed at online Vietnam Wall sites: multiple fragmentation wounds; artillery — rocket or mortar; air loss — crash on land; vehicle crash, accidental homicide, disease, and one termed "misadventure." The most common listing, and one that marks this as a true guerrilla war, was "small arms fire."

The Wall doesn't include the names of soldiers who later succumbed to cancer due to Agent Orange or the many soldiers who committed suicide due to post-traumatic stress. It is estimated that two or more entire Walls would be needed to carry these names. The estimates of suicides by soldiers returning from Vietnam are as high as 50,000.

Approximately one million Vietnamese combatants and three to four million Vietnamese civilians died in the Vietnam War. Like the 58,245 American soldiers on the Wall, each one was a brother, a sister, a son, a daughter. Some were fathers, some were mothers, many were children.

The east and west walls of the memorial together cover a distance of 494 feet. If the names of four million Vietnamese were memorialized on such a wall, it would run for six and a half miles.

In 2000, eighteen years after the dedication of the Wall, Maya Lin wrote in "Making the Memorial" in the *New York Review of Books*:

> On a personal level, I wanted to focus on the nature of accepting and coming to terms with a loved one's death. Simple as it may seem, I remember feeling that accepting a person's death is the first step in being able to overcome that loss.
>
> I felt that as a culture ... we were not willing or able to accept death or dying as a part of life.... In the design of the memorial, a fundamental goal was to be honest about death, since we must accept that loss in order to begin to overcome it. The pain of the loss will always be there, it will always hurt, but we must acknowledge the death in order to move on.

3

Memory

... the Iliad *was written not to glorify war (though it admits its fascination) but to emphasize its tragic futility.*
— E.V. Rieu, Introduction to Homer's The Iliad

Is it fair to make up the story of a man's life? We all make up our own pasts, in any case. For each of us our past is constructed of certain

Part 7

memories that stick, others that don't, or that stay for a while and then dissolve like the day's clouds. We choose to remember (or can't help but remember) certain events, particular faces, specific places, and we let others go. In the novel *Mansfield Park*, Jane Austen called it "the inequalities of memory." What we remember, the fragments we recall, are what we use to construct our past, our story. It is a made thing and highly selective.

Our memories are astonishingly limited. Lewis Carroll had the Queen voice one of memory's limits in *Alice Through the Looking Glass* when she said: "It's a poor sort of memory that only works backwards." The faces I've forgotten could people another world filled with cities of a million souls.

Nostalgia is one form of memory. Gabriel García Márquez, in his memoir *Living to Tell the Tale*, writes that nostalgia wipes away bad memories and magnifies good ones. Yet the words *memory* and *nostalgia* share a distinct negative connotation. The root sources of the word *memory* are linked with a slew of Indo-European words that express grief, mourning, sadness, anxiety, sorrow, doubt, and regret. (The Old English *murnan* means "to grieve.")

Nostalgia, too, has negative connotations in its root form. It combines the Greek *nostos*, "a return home," with the Greek word *algia*, or "pain."

The ancient Greeks depicted in *The Iliad* knew much about the "pain" of being unable to "return home." (And, of course, Ulysses knew the great struggle involved in returning home and the pain of what he found there.) The first work of literature in the Western world focuses on this subject, as well as on the nature of war. The Trojan Wars have stood as our template for the "tragic futility" of war ever since.

When I was nine years old, my oldest brother gave me a beautifully illustrated child's copy of *The Iliad and the Odyssey* (A Giant Golden Book, Deluxe Edition), inscribing it, "In hopes that from this you may learn to love the literature of the ancients."

Two images in the book stand out from my memories of childhood. On page 36 the funeral of the Greek warrior, Patroclus, best friend of Achilles, is illustrated. Five black-clad women carry the body of Patroclus on a bier on their shoulders, while others stand nearby wailing. And on page 44 the nude body of the great Trojan warrior, Hector, lies in the dust outside the city. A handful of women can be seen wailing on the city walls in the distance. Achilles, who killed Hector, shamelessly cuts the tendons behind his ankles and threads leather thongs through them. He attaches Hector to his chariot and proceeds to drag him through the dust beneath the towering walls of Troy before the eyes of his parents, his wife, his children.

Two fine young men. One from each side. Dead. Dead. A Greek father and a Trojan mother both weep.

It is eerily quiet. The city of Troy has fallen, following the appearance of the great horse that, in fact, hid Greek soldiers inside it, that poisonous gift (oddly, the German word for poison is *das gift*) that has echoed down through history. The last line of *The Iliad*, in this version, reads: "And the bodies of her [Troy's] children lay scattered in great numbers in the streets and houses — even in the very temples themselves."

The line sparks memories of scenes from Vietnam: jungle villages, dead children, dead soldiers both American and Vietnamese, shattered Buddhist temples. And a great weeping in America, a great weeping in Vietnam, a great weeping in Germany and Japan and Iraq and many other places, too many places. A great weeping followed by a great quiet.

Perhaps it is a blessing that we can sometimes forget.

Part 8

1
Circle

OVER THE YEARS THE Farm became a rough microcosm of the Canadian multicultural tapestry as people from a number of countries and Canadian provinces moved there. We didn't attract any Vietnamese, Chinese, or Jamaicans, but the population ended up including a pair of Germans, a number of Anglos from Ontario, three French-speaking Québécois, one Anglo-Quebecker, an Englishwoman, and several former Americans.

One of the first arrivals from overseas was Jochen, a German who Wally and I had met in Munich at the Oktoberfest in 1967. A less Prussian-like German could hardly be imagined. Jochen was a gentle soul who could learn just about any skill in a short time. Leaving behind a job as a bank clerk in Frankfurt, he moved to Canada and came to live at the Farm. He arrived, trudging across the fields in his favourite black velvet pants, a nimbus of blond hair around his head.

While living at my place, Jochen set to work fixing up a small, long-abandoned log cabin at the far end of the Farm that had once held a family of six early in the century and had later been converted into a granary. It was in rough shape but soon blossomed into a livable space under his care and attention. Jochen planted a garden and settled in.

Jochen had a spring by the stream where he fetched his drinking water, and one day he noticed that a tiny trout had swum into his spring box. He decided to pamper and feed the little trout which, over a few months, grew into a good-size adult fish. He would go to the spring box every day and visit with this trout and talk to it. Some days it was the only thing that he had to talk to. A great attachment grew between man and fish.

Then a visitor from Germany, Harold, who looked like a youthful cross between Albert Einstein and Leon Trotsky, arrived to stay with Jochen. First time in Canada, first time in the wilderness. The day after

Harold arrived, the wood stove in Jochen's cabin and its chimney caught fire, flames shooting out of the stove. Jochen, busy beating back the flames, yelled at Harold to take the bucket, go to the spring box, and fetch water. The last thing Jochen said was, "Watch out for the fish," but Harold's English was minimal and he didn't really understand. Moments later he was back and threw a full bucket of water on the stove, the fish landing on the still-hot grill. At first Jochen was so busy dealing with flames and smoke that he didn't notice the fish wriggling and grilling on top of the stove. Then he saw it. "My fish!" he shouted.

"Mein Gott!" exclaimed Harold.

It was too late. Jochen's trout was done in. When the fire was out, Harold apologized over and over. Jochen, dangling the trout by the tail, shrugged back tears. Then they had a laugh together and ate the fish.

Soon Jochen met a Québécois nurse, Monik, who moved out to the Farm to join him. She spoke only French and he spoke German and a smattering of English, but somehow, through music and gardening, they were able to overcome these language barriers. I always picture Jochen "tilting at windmills," or perhaps I should say, getting his windmills to tilt. Wind and solar power fascinated him, at least until electricity came to the Farm in the 1980s. He was always building windmill towers out of bits and pieces of the world's detritus such as parts of old dead automobiles, of which there was a steady supply at the Farm. Jochen, like all the men at the Farm, often worked as a carpenter, building decks, replacing roofs, and so on.

Eventually, Jochen started a stained-glass studio in the barn with another German, Fritz, who arrived from Cologne, son of a nursery owner and an exceptional gardener. We christened the studio the Glass Forest Workshop and set to work on a steady supply of orders for stained-glass windows and lamps. Like almost everyone who moved to the Farm, Fritz lived for a short while in my cabin but then built his own house. He didn't quite build it from scratch, however. While he was working at a carpentry job near Wakefield, a wooden cottage became available free for the moving. With the help of other people living on the Farm, Fritz chainsawed the wooden walls of the entire cottage into eight sections, loaded them onto a flatbed truck, and moved it to the Farm, situating it in a pleasant location in the woods above the stream. After building a platform, we stood the sections up, spliced them together, and, presto, a house. Truthfully, there was quite a bit more work involved, but the house was soon livable. And then Rita, another Québécois woman, moved in with Fritz.

Shortly after the arrival of the Germans, Dave and Val moved to the Farm. They joined me in my cabin, bought into the property, and began work on an eight-sided log cabin of their own in a field down the road from me. Dave was a Quebecker, long, lanky and strong, who walked with a swagger. He worked hard (another carpenter), liked his beer, and could play a mean game of chess. Val, his partner, had grown up on a farm near Oxford, England. She was salt of the earth, with her green thumbs inserted deep in the soil of her flourishing garden. Val possessed such fine artistic skills that for a while she made a living sewing fancy bridal gowns, and later as an artist.

Jochen and Monik, Fritz and Rita, Dave and Val, Paul and Colleen, and I became regulars at the sauna gatherings and other social events that were part of life at the Farm. Then Steve, who had split with Shirley, moved back to the Farm and brought a woman named Rini (short for Loreen), originally from Cape Breton. They tore down a partially wrecked cabin in one of the Farm's distant fields and rebuilt it nearby in another field at the foot of the rock face that overlooked the Farm. Meanwhile, Paul and Colleen (with their little girl, Oona), deciding their original place was too small for their needs, began work on a larger house on a small rise in the same field as my own place. Suddenly, the sauna was getting crowded.

The main forms of entertainment when we socialized at the Farm were conversation and music. The conversation always split into two well-defined groups. In one room of the cabin, usually the kitchen (the early parties were often at my place), the men sat around in overalls or jeans, flannel shirts, and work boots, drinking beer and talking about tractors (how we should all chip in for one for the Farm and how much work it could save and where they had seen one for sale in Wakefield or Masham), or cars (what's broken, how to fix it, where to get another cheap one), or other engines and machines such as windmills and pumps. Few of our ever-present fantasies and dreams were realized due to a persistent lack of funds.

In the other room of the cabin — the living room with its two small dusty couches and the rocking chair I had bought in Amish country in central Ohio and refinished years before — the women, drinking wine or beer, wearing overalls or jeans and work boots, talked about gardens or cooking or, occasionally, books, and (eventually) children. I appeared to be the one who mostly moved from one group to the other. When the men's discussion proved too technical or argumentative or boring, I moved over to listen to the women. If the women's talk proved disagreeable, I moved back to the men. Sometimes I just went for a walk.

But usually I waited for the music to start. Music was germane to our life at the Farm. Music and food and gardens were what drew us together, but music in particular seemed to join us on a more profound and instinctual level. (Not everyone always felt that way — Fritz, who didn't play an instrument, eventually seemed to lose patience with the way music hijacked every gathering.) But for most of the Farm dwellers, music was a basic means of expressing our enjoyment at being together.

Not that we were all particularly good musicians. Jochen played guitar, as did Dave. Steve, the most serious musician among us, played the flute and saxophone. Meanwhile, Paul was trying to learn the mandolin. Early on we had made him practise up in the chicken house when the scratching began to drive us crazy. I played the harmonica, with the famous saying of Orson Welles always troubling my mind: "He has Van Gogh's ear for music." Almost everyone took a turn at dulcimer and spoons and singing, with the slim, pretty Cape Bretoner, Rini, having the best voice.

The thing that really drew us together, though, was drumming. There were times when we would begin a spontaneous collective drum and percussion session that would end up in a kind of hypnotic group ecstasy with everyone banging on or shaking whatever was handy, including pot lids, pots, tabletops, spoons and knives, glasses, plates, bottles, gourd rattles and scrapers, tambourines, and genuine drums (Steve had built a set out of two-foot-high hollow logs, and there always seemed to be other drums about.) A frenetic full-blown session could go on for an hour or more with almost everyone taking part. From the outside I'm sure it sounded like a prolonged fourteen-vehicle car crash, but being involved in it was cathartic. Of course, our ecstasies were augmented not only with

Part 8

beer and wine but usually with homegrown pot and hashish, as well.

In *A Dictionary of Symbols,* J.E. Cirlot writes: "With the aid of drums, shamans can induce a state of ecstasy." It is said that the drum is the "shaman's horse" because the shaman uses it to enter an altered state of consciousness. The word *shaman* is originally from the Russian and is linked to the Prakrit (Indic) word *samana,* "Buddhist monk," "mendicant," or "ascetic." Another old synonym for shaman was "diabolical artist." The word also means "to heat up, to burn." Drumming together seemed to bring a sense of catharsis and release to our heated-up gatherings. Without realizing it we seemed to be instinctively expressing age-old ways of working with community.

Today, although we haven't drummed together in years, the faint echo of a great ruckus is still barely discernible inside the old cabin's wooden walls.

2
Wheels

I think that cars today are almost the exact equivalent of the great Gothic cathedrals: I mean the supreme creation of an era, conceived with passion by unknown artists, and consumed in image if not in usage by a whole population which appropriates them as a purely magical object.

It is obvious that the new Citroën has fallen from the sky.... The D.S. ("Diesse") — the "Goddess" — has all the features of one of those objects from another universe....

— Roland Barthes, "The New Citroën," Mythologies

IN MY EARLIEST TIMES at the Farm, I lived without transportation of any kind — no car, no bicycle, no access to a bus. My feet and legs took me the several miles into Wolf Lake and back for groceries and whatever else I needed. A few friends, however, did own automobiles, including Ron, an American friend from New York and Vermont with a bushy moustache who spent part of one winter living with me in the earliest years at the cabin, and who drove a large Citroën D.S. from the mid-1960s. It was freakish-looking (what would one expect of a car whose name has an umlaut?), a vehicle only the French would or could build: low-slung, long, sleek, ultra-modern, like something out of Jean-Luc Godard's futuristic film *Alphaville*. This monster had a hydraulic suspension, which meant it could be raised about a foot higher on its wheels with the flick of a switch. This proved to be highly useful in hauling goods, such as cordwood or building supplies, across the field, over the stream, and right up to the front door of the cabin. Unfortunately, the hydraulic fluid leaked and was expensive. In true country style, we found that Mazola corn oil worked just as well at a tenth of the price.

The first car I bought while living at the Farm was the aforementioned 1947 Chevy, which belonged to a spinster in Wakefield who had been its first and only owner. Thin and frail, wearing a worn flower-patterned dress that may have been as aged as the car, the woman took me out to her tumbledown garage to have a look. She pulled the garage doors open and we stared at the car's smooth, rounded back end.

"She runs fine." Turning, thin lips pursed, she gave me her serious, all-business look. "I'll want $200 for it."

I drove it home, the proud owner of a six-passenger, two-door Chevrolet Town Sedan, "a five-window coach with built-in trunk" (what other kind of trunk is there?), all the while luxuriating in the dove-grey seats that looked and felt like velvet and were hardly worn. The steering wheel was enormous, larger than one you would find today in a semi-trailer.

In 1947, with the Second World War still a recent memory in the minds of North Americans, the colours offered for the 1947 Chevy included Battleship Grey and Freedom Blue, as well as Lakeside Green, Oxford Maroon, and the suspiciously Canadian-sounding Maple Brown. My new old car was black.

Money was still tight in those early postwar years. The prosperous 1950s and the free-spending 1960s hadn't arrived yet. A 1947 advertisement for "The Newest Chevrolet" reads: "Big-Car Quality at

Lowest Cost." And, in smaller print at the bottom of the ad: "It's bigger-looking, better-looking, and the most <u>beautiful buy</u> in its field." (The underlining appears in the original.)

I soon discovered that my old car had what I thought was a rather newfangled innovation — cruise control. When the Chevy was up to speed, there was a lever one could pull out from the dashboard to keep the vehicle steadily cruising. At least that was the idea. With the cruise control engaged, the car tended to slow down considerably on the smallest hill. But on the flat, it was a dream.

There was certainly something "1940s" about the look of the car. Round, round, and round. And it was huge. Each headlight stared out from a long, sweeping panel that resembled a one-eyed leopard in mid-leap; the extended hood looked like the bulbous nose of a medium-size whale, while the grille was a shark with multiple sets of teeth.

It ran smoothly, the engine seemed young still, but getting it to stop was an iffy proposition. Luckily, those were the days when the Province of Quebec didn't require drivers to carry insurance of any kind. I would almost certainly have needed it because the brake lines on the car squirted fluid at every application of the brakes. I worked on them, but nothing plugged the holes. After I owned the car about eight months and had dumped gallons of brake fluid, I was driving with a few friends in Ottawa when we were stopped in a roadside safety check. Not only did my vehicle not pass the check, I was given a ticket for driving with only one functional brake.

Surprisingly, the officer let me drive the car home after I pleaded my case and agreed to have the problem fixed. When I took it to a garage a few days later, I learned that the Chevy was nearly an official antique (cars become antiques at thirty years) and the necessary parts would have to be ordered from a special supplier in Chicago at a cost far exceeding the original price I had paid for the car. So I sold it — for fifteen bucks to a young local who lived in a shack on the road into Wolf Lake.

I was so inexperienced in the ways of the world that I left the plates on for the new owner. The next evening a brave and helpful young woman knocked on the door of my cabin and told me her cousin and his friends were planning to do stupid things in the car while my name was still officially attached to it. So I went to his shack and unscrewed the plates from the old Chev under the stares of a crowd that was in the midst of a drinking party. I guess they were planning to rob a bank or something. If I were going to rob a bank, I don't think I'd want a highly visible '47 Chevy as my getaway car, especially one that could barely stop.

In the early years at the Farm, I was also given two VW Beetles at different times. One was from my eldest brother and his wife, Bud and Ann, and the second came from my friends, Paul and Colleen. Neither car was in great shape, but the generosity of these friends and relations was commendable. In both cases I attempted to do as much of the repair work as possible myself. This was an endless, and largely fruitless, task. I was even worse as a mechanic than I was as a carpenter. Occasionally, I had a minor success fixing something, but more often than not I broke more things than I fixed and was always in serious danger of poking myself in the eye.

I recall driving one Beetle all winter with no heat or defrost, which was no mean feat in Canada. Driving became a project that involved one hand on the wheel and the other with a scraper constantly cleaning a space the size of a postcard on the windshield. Another time I drove the Bug for several weeks using only the emergency brake to stop because the regular brakes had ceased functioning entirely.

Then there was the great spark plug fiasco. It was summer. The Beetle wouldn't start, so Paul, Steve, and I replaced the spark plugs. We were using a VW repair book for dummies. The details describing how to run the spark plug wires from the plugs to the distributor cap were given in a block of text in the book. Paul, who was a crackerjack sketch artist, drew a helpful illustration in the margin of the page showing the pattern, for which we were all grateful because it meant there was no need to pore over the text each time we wanted to check the wiring details.

For weeks we pushed the VW up and down the dirt road, popping the clutch to try to start it. It would cough and splutter and spit ... and die. Over and over, seemingly for eight hours a day, we pushed it back and forth, determined to conquer this small beast and make it work.

It became an obsession among the men on the Farm. How could this minor mechanical mystery defeat us? We were intelligent, skilled in matters mechanistic (some of us more skilled than others); we would not, could not, give up. We checked everything else: the battery was good, no problem with starter or solenoid.

But there was one small problem we had consistently overlooked. Paul's neat and concise drawing in the margin of the book contained a slight error. Everyone had taken for granted that we had correctly connected the wires, because we had checked it a dozen times a day — checked it, that is, against Paul's sketch, not against the original text.

Finally, I noticed that the illustration didn't quite match the words. "Hey, Paul," I said, pointing at the now-grimy page in the manual, "are you sure this drawing is right?" He checked. We changed the wires, and the VW started right up.

Both VWs served to keep me mobile for a while before they rusted out or blew up or got too dangerous to drive. In the end, they made great planters.

People who gave me things, like cars, were always disappointed when I didn't take good care of them — but I simply didn't have the money. Nor did I have the skills (innate or learned), though I worked as much as I could on all my cars. But, after an afternoon of frustration, always lacking the right tools (which were expensive), I'd throw my hands up in frustration and disgust and go for a calming walk in the woods, or read a book, or write a poem.

Most of the cars we drove at the Farm were unconditional wrecks, and we all had intriguing tales to tell. Jochen once got a deal on a blue Ford pickup truck — only $75. The fact that it didn't go into reverse wasn't a deal breaker. He bought it, anyway, and was careful how he parked.

The other German at the farm, Fritz, once left his large dog, Bozo, a German shepherd–Labrador mix, locked in his car one afternoon while he went to visit with friends. In the depths of his boredom and loneliness, the poor beast proceeded to chew off about a two-foot-square section from the middle of the padded dashboard.

Another time several of us were headed into town, Fritz driving his yellow Pontiac convertible. I was seated next to him and Steve was in the back, our long hair blowing in the wind. The Quebec Provincial Police stopped us on the highway about ten miles from Ottawa.

"Open the trunk," the policeman said.

The trunk was tied down with wire because it wouldn't hold otherwise. It took me about ten minutes to unwind all the wires, and when I pushed it open, a questioning look crossed the cop's face because the trunk was loaded with rocks. "For traction on the snow," I explained, realizing how ridiculous that sounded since it was summer and we had been driving with the top down. We had never bothered to take the rocks out since the previous winter. The cop shook his head in disbelief.

The policeman asked for our identifications and told Steve to get out of the back seat and present his ID, as well. When Steve stood up in the back of the convertible, he went straight through the floorboards and was standing in the road! The cop shook his head again. Steve climbed out, opened his wallet, and a joint of marijuana rolled onto the ground. Luckily, at that moment, I was handing my own driver's licence to the cop, so he didn't notice the reefer because he was turning to me. Steve stepped on the joint, and the rest of the interview was conducted with him going in circles, only able to move one foot.

One of the last cars I owned at the Farm was a British Rover T2000 from the late 1960s, with all-leather interior, toggle switches on the dashboard, and four on the floor. Although it was cool beyond belief, it was still a wreck. I could only afford to buy and maintain it because my wife, Janet, had taken a job in the city. I felt like a stud driving it; like James Bond but with better literary taste. It was British racing green, a hip-sounding colour if there ever was one.

Janet was commuting to her job, so the car had to start throughout the winter. No matter how cold the morning, it always started, unlike many of the other vehicles at the Farm. With other cars we all became experts at placing a metal baking dish of hot coals under the oil pan in order to warm the oil enough to possibly, just maybe, turn the engine over; we became experts at the positive/negative science of booster cables; learned that a frozen battery can explode while being boosted; discovered many things we hadn't previously known about starting cars in the frozen wastes of the north. And we always learned the hard way. But not with the Rover — at minus forty-five degrees Fahrenheit it started with ease.

Part 8

But I also learned that fancy foreign cars cost a fortune to keep on the road. I often took the Rover into a garage in Ottawa where the Jamaican mechanics were rough experts, always joking, as they informed me it would take three weeks to get a simple part or as they presented me with a bill that tore my heart out through my wallet. With the outrageous cost of repairs, I didn't know whether to laugh with them or weep.

3
Bust

IT COULDN'T LAST. WE were having entirely too good a time. The marijuana plants in the garden that summer were glorious. Having been started indoors in the early spring by a friend, the eight plants had had a good head start on the season. Under a strong summer sun, and just the right amount of rain, they grew to a height of ten feet by mid-August. Continual snipping of the branches allowed them to bush out into six-foot-diameter behemoths around the middle. I had planted them in the garden's prime location, with its richest, softest loam and, unfortunately, visible from the road.

When harvest time came in early autumn, I dried the plants by hanging them upside down on the back of the cabin where they stretched from the roofline almost to the ground. Once they were dry, I stripped the leaves off and shoved them into a garbage bag, ready to smoke my way through a full year's supply of weed. I hid the bag in a doghouse directly behind the cabin, a ploy that eventually proved to be less than brilliant.

My girlfriend, Janet, enjoyed pot as much as I did, spending an inordinate amount of time in the long evenings drawing abstract images with coloured pencils, hiding behind her veil of long dark hair. We were planning to marry the coming December.

In early October we were cooking breakfast one quiet morning when I happened to glance out the window. There, walking up the trail toward the cabin, was a handful of police officers. I stared blankly for a moment, uncomprehending. Then it hit me, and I swallowed a breath. In one swift motion I thrust the basket of pot on the table into the fire box and replaced the iron lid on the stove. A moment later I heard a determined knock on the door. Janet's eyes were as big and startled as the two fried eggs quickly hardening in the frying pan on the stove.

I answered the door, my heart throbbing in my throat and my legs gone wobbly. A Quebec Provincial Police officer thrust a search warrant into my hand and entered. We were told to wait in the kitchen while they searched the house. About ten minutes later an officer came back downstairs after finding no pot or any other drugs for that matter, and commented on my Buddhist shrine: "Ya inta voodoo or what?"

A moment later another officer came proudly in from behind the cabin holding a garbage bag full of pot as if he had just shot a brace of hare. "Hah!" he announced. I was dismayed. How in the world did I think stashing a plastic garbage bag of illegal substances in the doghouse ten feet behind the cabin was an excellent hiding place? My own foolishness was biting me in the tail. My own pot was, apparently, making me stupid.

The QPP officers checked the other houses on the property, as well, including those belonging to Paul, Jochen, and Fritz (the two Germans and Paul had by now built their own places). The police found small amounts of pot at all these locations. A search of Dave and Val's eight-sided log cabin was aborted when the brave officers were scared off by the bees from Dave's nearby hives.

Four of us were charged with a variety of infractions, mine being the most serious, as the bounty of my garden translated into more fulsome charges. The Quebec police obviously remained untouched by the inroads of 1960s feminism, since none of the females (each of us had a girlfriend living with us) in any of the houses of ill pot repute were charged. I was taken to a distant police station to be photographed ("turn to the side, please") and fingerprinted. Everyone was friendly, and many of the people I had to deal with seemed somewhat embarrassed to be going through all of this rigmarole for growing a little pot.

Some months later a knock came on the back door of the cabin quite early in the morning in the middle of winter. The snow was head high, and I couldn't imagine who could be knuckling my door at such an early hour. I leaped out of bed and answered, only to be handed a summons by the silent knocker who was probably terrified out of his skull wondering what he might encounter at such a time and in such a place ("axe-wielding maniac" had probably passed through his mind). He immediately turned around and hightailed it out of there, his work done, our fated face-to-face moment over before it began.

According to the papers he had handed me, I was charged with possession, growing, and selling of marijuana. It was time to hire a lawyer. Being convicted of selling marijuana at that time could have brought me a possible sentence of seven years in jail (although actual sentences for pot were much milder, almost never leading to jail time). An acquaintance gave me the name of a lawyer in Hull who agreed to handle my case.

Several months later, on a sunny winter's day, four of us from the Farm — Paul, Jochen, Fritz, and I — were required to appear at the provincial courthouse in the sleepy town of Shawville, Quebec, about twenty miles away. After waiting in the overheated hallway of the old three-storey building, we were called into the courtroom where we took our places on the shiny wooden benches along with a variety of other "criminals." High windows streamed with morning light, the brilliance of which did nothing to lighten our sombre moods. After we listened to His Honour passing judgment on several illegal fishermen and hunters, all of whom seemed to be poor rural people who didn't quite understand what they were doing in court, our case came up.

The judge, seated on his high dais, appeared to be in his early forties and had a kind-looking face. When the police officer explained that they had found such and such an amount of illegal marijuana at our Farm, the judge asked, "And where is the marijuana now?"

The officer smiled broadly. "We burned it, Your Honour."

"I see." The judge was grinning. "And were you careful not to stand downwind, Officer?"

Everyone in the courtroom laughed, including the policeman, who didn't bother answering.

My lawyer asked for more time to prepare the case, and the judge agreed to a delay (first cheque to the lawyer). Then it was delayed again two months later (second cheque to the lawyer), and delayed again four months after that (third cheque to the lawyer). For the next hearing my incompetent lawyer didn't even bother to show up.

The judge was angry and told the police to work out a deal as soon as possible. I was referred to a fresh-faced legal-aid lawyer who suggested that my previous lawyer was a criminal himself who loved to drag cases out as long as possible so he could bleed his clients. From his office the legal-aid lawyer called the police. "Listen, this case has been going on for over a year. Can't we let him plead to a lesser charge and get it over with?"

The trafficking charge was dropped, I pleaded guilty to possessing and growing marijuana, and was given a $200 fine. But that year of waiting was twelve long months filled with anguish. The unknown, fuelled by the powerful fantasies of the imagination, is truly the worst of all punishments. I felt like Raskolnikov in Fyodor Dostoevsky's *Crime and Punishment*. One ends up imagining the worst possible scenario and living through it mentally over and over. I decided I didn't enjoy my dealings with Jean Law or the justice system and promptly stopped smoking pot from the day of the bust forward.

It was a good thing, too, because the Farm was raided again six months later, this time by the RCMP, and for completely different reasons.

It was autumn, a lovely day, warm enough to work outside in a flannel shirt. I was behind the cabin with a load of firewood in my arms when I heard a strange sound in the field out front. Coming around the cabin, I was amazed to see three cars travelling at high speed, pounding across the field and up to my front door, bouncing over the corrugated meadow like three speedboats on rough seas. Instantly, a giant in jeans and a sports shirt appeared before me. He must have been six foot six and three feet wide at the shoulders. I stared at him. "Who ... who are you?" I stammered.

"RCMP. Put your hands up."

I dropped the wood and put my hands in the air. *Not again*, I thought. *Thank God I'm clean.*

He patted me down, mumbling, "Jeez, there's nothing to you. You're skin and bone." He stood up as other plainclothes officers and a few in uniforms appeared behind him. "Any weapons in the house?"

Part 8

Still stunned, I shook my head. "I don't own any guns."

"Any drugs?"

I guess they were trying to catch me off guard while my head was still spinning. "No. No, nothing. None." And it was true, although they didn't seem to believe me.

Twelve officers went through my house thoroughly. They also searched around the house (the doghouse was blessedly empty this time) and looked down every trail that disappeared into the forest from the surrounding fields. Then they searched the other houses on the Farm and found no drugs there, either. While they were searching my house, I was taken by an officer up to Paul and Colleen's house and was told to sit in a wooden chair in the middle of Paul's kitchen. An investigator, dressed in a suit, entered carrying a briefcase. He was about forty years old, with close-cropped hair, and had the look of a military officer — all business. Unsnapping the briefcase and opening it, he removed a sheet of paper, which he handed to me. "What is this?" he demanded.

I glanced at the sheet of paper in my hand and blinked. I was staring at an unfamiliar, handmade map that sketched how to get from the village of Wakefield to the Farm, this Farm, my Farm. "It's a map to the Farm."

He walked in circles around me and stood behind my chair. "Who drew it?"

"I have no idea."

"Did you draw it?"

"No, I didn't. I really don't know where it came from or what its purpose is."

"This map was found in the house of a big-time drug smuggler who we just arrested in Wakefield — and it points to this Farm. We believe there's a hidden cache of smuggled drugs on this property. Why else would he have a map to your Farm? And you say you know nothing about it?"

"Nothing." I shook my head, dumbfounded. A thousand possibilities were flashing through my mind. *Maybe someone from Wakefield did hide drugs here.* I knew a few rough characters in the nearby village, but I kept my distance from them, especially since my own bust. *Maybe someone on the Farm knows about it. Maybe I'm really in big trouble this time. But*

I know nothing about it. A map to here? Why? No answer leaped to the front of my brain.

He asked me a few more questions, always circling about my chair, then went to the door and called in an officer to take me outside. "Wait with this officer." He addressed another policeman in the yard. "Bring in the other one."

They brought Paul in and sat him down in the chair I had just vacated. The young officer led me outside, where we sat on logs next to each other overlooking the field. After staring out at the field and the surrounding hills for a while, a few birds calling in the distance, the policeman said, "I could get used to a place like this. It's nice and quiet around here."

I agreed, and we sat in companionable silence, waiting.

After interviewing Paul and learning nothing new, the police showed the map to other people on the Farm. Paul and I waited under guard while the mysterious map made its way to the doors of our neighbours. Finally, our friend and fellow farm member, Dave, recognized it and owned up as being the artist of the map.

Dave explained that a number of us on the Farm had started a craft workshop in the barn the previous year, dealing mostly in wooden objects, furniture, and stained-glass objects. Dave had given the map to the Wakefield drug dealer because the latter had shown an interest in coming out to the Farm to buy some crafts (drug dealers, too, need Christmas gifts!) and he needed directions. It soon became apparent that the RCMP had let their imaginations run wild when they stumbled across the map, seeing a drug smuggler under every rock and a pusher behind every tree. The policemen had a good laugh. We all let out a great sigh of relief. And no one at the Farm was charged.

After the police left, Paul called me into his kitchen where he and I had been interviewed. We were still wiping the sweat from our brows and thanking our lucky stars and moons. He opened a bottle of beer for me and took one for himself. The impish Paul gave me a crooked smile and shook his head. "I can't believe it," he said, lifting a wide-brimmed leather hat from the kitchen counter for me to see. Underneath was a plastic baggie stuffed with dried pot. "They never looked under the hat."

Part 8

4
Chagall's Cabin: September 2004

ON A RECENT TRIP to Venice with my second wife, Faith, we visit the Peggy Guggenheim Museum where I happen upon an intriguing painting by Marc Chagall, who was from Vitebsk, a town in Belarus about ninety miles northeast of Borisov. Chagall, who was born in 1889, lived in Belarus until he moved to Paris in 1910. For a few years Simon and Chagall shared a similar culture and geography.

The painting *La Pluie* (*Rain*) depicts a small, sturdy cabin of squared logs that bears a striking resemblance to my place in the Gatineau Hills. Chagall, who based the work on his recollections of childhood, painted it a short time after arriving in Paris. It offers the free-flowing associations and images typical of Chagall's work: memories, strong, simple colours, overlapping times, interpenetration of dream worlds and reality, ordinary people and animals.

I could be looking at a scene I know intimately. A man, perhaps drunk, teeters at the side of the house. Beyond him stands a barn with a small, friendly-looking horse inside. In the sky above, another man tends a goat, or is perhaps about to butcher it. A pair of potted plants in the cabin's window lean out toward the rain. A man exits the front door carrying an umbrella. Four steps lead up to the cabin's front door, above which are the letters ABK. Could these be the owner's initials? The simplicity reminds me of the church in Wolf Lake with its name indicated in capital letters: ST-FRS-D'ASS.

The tilt of the cabin makes it appear to be floating, as if it were a house in a dream.

One of the first things I made for myself when I moved to the country was a ladder. I used two dead spruce trees with their limbs removed and hammered round rungs between them. The result was a rough ladder that I always left leaning up against the cabin. Ladders figure prominently in Chagall's work. A ladder inevitably appears when he addresses any

Christian or biblical theme. He uses the ladder image in a number of paintings, including *Jacob's Ladder* and *Jacob's Dream*. Jacob, the traditional ancestor of all Israel, had a dream of angels going up and down a ladder to heaven. The ladder also represents the ancestral line Jacob founded.

The ladder also figures in the world of the shaman. Once a shaman has fallen into a trance from drumming and dancing, he symbolically connects heaven and earth by climbing a tree, a post, or a ladder.

In Chagall it seems to me the ladder also stands for the artist's idea of escape, of exile. Only the artist can escape by going up, into heaven, into the creative, instead of out and down. The artist can free himself by seeking exile among the stars where, like a *saltimbanque* of the night skies, he can travel from one star to another over tightropes of light.

I picture Chagall perched on the peak of my cabin, an easel before him, a brush in one hand, his own head playfully in the other. It's the middle of night. He leans out and dabs the black sky with his brush — sequins of stars appear. With a flick of the wrist he paints a crescent moon, and with a light-handed swish the Milky Way appears trailing from his brush.

Looking closely at the easel, I see it is empty. He could paint anything there — as an artist, he could create any world he desires.

I liken his empty easel to my world as an exile. (Chagall too, like Simon and me, was an exile.) Like a voluntary exile, a traveller without a home, I feel free to wander anywhere my interest or curiosity takes me, to find inspiration in anything the phenomenal world reveals. In that sense the artist is never in exile but always at home in the world.

In fact, I can honestly claim I have never felt like an exile. Of course, in my case, I was soon able to go back to the United States if I wanted and Canada is similar in many ways to the United States. In fact, when I came to Canada, I felt as if I were coming home.

I want to say that home, in any case, was wherever my books were, but even that isn't true. If I had a small notebook and a pen in my pocket with which I could jot notes and observations, I was at home, at home in language, as if the interlacing of the words formed a nest of sorts, a place to rest, a place that was familiar. And from that nest on the roof I could look out on heaven and earth and, pen in hand, write myself a world.

Part 8

5
Portrait

I STARE AT A photograph of the grandfather I never met. Simon died three years before I was born, and my own father never liked to talk about him. The pain and anger at having been abandoned as a child was too deeply felt. In the photo Simon is sixty-four years of age. Three years later, in 1944, he would die on an unseasonably hot spring day in New York City.

Simon, nearly bald and wearing round, rimless eyeglasses, stares directly into the camera. His perfectly round head, softened by a pleasingly straight jaw, is tilted at a slight angle. He wears a tweed three-piece suit, a handsome tie tucked into the top of his vest. The way the tie's knot fits perfectly into the *V* of the collar of his white shirt marks him as a careful, conservative dresser and reveals his early profession as a tailor. A small, well-trimmed moustache also points to a man who was impeccable in regards to his personal appearance.

In the photo Simon stares at me from the past, from more than half a century ago. I try to read what is in the eyes of this man whose blood is in my veins as surely as silt invisibly drifts in the Berezina River. There is a resignation to the look of the eyes in the photo, and in the thin mouth, too, which appears to hover on a line balanced between bitterness and humour. This seems quintessentially Jewish — the deep historical sufferings of a people and the saving grace of humour all in one man.

And one can easily see why those eyes projected sorrow and that narrow mouth tilted toward bitterness. The tragedies of his life were legion. It seemed that he was visited by blow after blow, each of which must have tested his strength and, possibly, ensured his ultimate resilience. There were times when all he could do was lie in the dark and stare. Despite these sorrows and tremendous losses — the deaths of his first wife and two young daughters in the collapse of the building in Cleveland, the loss of home and family as an exile — he loved the simple pleasures of life:

dressing up for parties, taking a piece of herring with a shot of Scotch before dinner, imagining the lives of passersby from a bench where he sat with his third wife in New York City.

He had a strong distaste for religion of all kinds, regarding it as superstitious and irrational. This likely stemmed from his disgust with his childhood Jewish school and its brutal teachers. In later life he avidly read freethinkers such as Colonel Robert Ingersoll, a famous anti-religious writer at the turn of the twentieth century, and the renowned anti-Bible lawyer, Clarence Darrow.

Simon celebrated the cultural traditions and Jewish holidays in order to appease his third wife, who had strong religious beliefs. During the Passover Seder, when it came time to make the ritual pronouncement, "Next year in Jerusalem," he would laugh and declare, "Next year we hope to be right here in America."

During a visit to my uncle's home in Virginia, we discuss my grandfather, his father, over gin and tonics. (Arnold was the youngest son from Simon's third marriage.) In the Second World War, Simon's oldest son, Leonard, and Arnold, were in the U.S. military. I wondered how Simon had felt about sending his sons off to war.

"When we went off to the military, he took it very hard. His health suffered. Of course, he had been a smoker [of cigars, never cigarettes] much of his life and had been told to stop. He had high blood pressure and developed angina, though I never saw him in pain.

"He had a couple of strokes while we were away and died of the last one after seeing both of us get back in time to his bedside. Not long before his last stroke, he said to me, 'I've been such an unsympathetic father.' Sometimes, yes, but I think I always understood that he carried huge burdens of sorrow and disappointment. His life was just a little more than he could handle.

"On his last day, as he lay in his bed, unable to talk at all and unable to move his left arm, I sat on the edge of the bed with him. It was hot in the New York apartment my parents then lived in — of course, there was no air conditioning in those days — and I was perspiring. With his one good arm, he lifted his sheet and wiped the perspiration off my face. There was enough love there to carry a whole childhood."

Part 8

6
Blue Log Cabin

CHAGALL, RECALLING HIS CHILDHOOD in Vitebsk, wrote in his autobiography *My Life* that he would often fear that the police were coming to take him away to join a regiment. He would hide under the bed at these times. While under the bed, he would dream of flying over the roofs of the village. When no policeman appeared, he came out of hiding, happy to still be a little boy and not a soldier. Later in the night he would dream of "policemen, soldiers, epaulettes, barracks."

In a comment on the Russian military as quoted in *Chagall by Chagall*, Chagall added: "... finding myself in the vicinity of army camps, my paints turned blue and my painting soured."

I wonder if, as a child, Simon dreamt of being stolen from his family and sent off to "the regiments." And I wonder if he thought of Borisov in the way that Chagall unhappily remembered Vitebsk (although the joy apparent in his paintings speaks otherwise). And I wonder if Simon looked at the clothes of the local herring seller and saw that they were speckled with scales, and if he thought then for the first time of the distant sea.

Like Chagall, he must have eaten black bread, meat with carrots, pickles, herring, cheese, noodles, meat broth, calf's-foot jelly, black kasha, and drank tea from a samovar. Perhaps, once in a while, he had a small glass of homemade brandy. Or maybe only when times were good. When times were bad, he probably ate nothing but black kasha, and drank tea that tasted as weak as Berezina river water.

In the old black-and-white photos, Belarus at the turn of the twentieth century appears to be a world without colour. Dull, dusty, bleak. And yet Chagall's paintings tell a different story: brilliant pigments shine out from a world rich with paradise-green horses, red-and-white cows, musicians with Chinese yellow beards holding yellow violins, blue log cabins, violet skies and ultramarine trees, bright emerald pigs.

7
Work

Long hair is a mark of a gentleman, for it is not easy to perform a plebeian task with long hair.

— *Aristotle*, Rhetoric

AMONG THE GREEKS, SURPRISINGLY, it was the Spartans (those warlike city dwellers whose name is synonymous with highly disciplined, stoic, clean living) who wore their hair long. And in *The Iliad*, the hardened Greek soldiers fighting against Troy are repeatedly referred to as "the long-haired Achaeans."

At the Farm all the males sported long hair of varying styles and lengths. I myself sometimes had hair that hung down well past the middle of my back. (When I moved to Ottawa years later, I asked an Italian barber, who had previously trimmed hair at the Vatican, to give my long locks a serious edit.) In some of the old photos I look more like an Apache than a former college kid from the suburbs. In others I resemble a Mexican bandito with a Zapatista moustache. In any case, what distinguished us from the Greeks was the essential headband.

Headbands, and toques in winter, were the necessary attire that made it possible to perform the endless "plebeian tasks" that were the main feature of life in the country. In fact, the entire back-to-the-land movement resembled, in odd ways, a kind of voluntary Maoist re-education plan — kids from the suburbs, for the most part, who were educated and well off, learning how the rural half lives.

Many of the tasks at the Farm involved bending over, in which case long hair falling in the face could be persistently annoying: gathering and cutting firewood, working in the garden, sweeping floors. It's interesting that so much manual labour is accomplished while staring down at the earth. In my case, soon after beginning one of these tasks, I would head into the cabin to grab a headband to control the tumbling hair. And there were an enormous number of tasks to accomplish.

I don't know how hippies got the reputation for being lazy, shiftless, work shirkers. While we couldn't be considered "stoic" like the Spartans, we were certainly hard working. The need to gather, cut, and split firewood became nearly a full-time job in late autumn and winter and included tasks such as stacking, carrying wood into the house, preparing kindling, building fires, emptying ashes from the stove, and cleaning chimneys.

In winter, work also revolved around the removal of snow. One needed a clear path to the outhouse, to the woodpile, and to the chopping block, to the compost heap, to the chicken house, down to the spring box, and so on. In my case, I also had a hundred-yard walk to the road, which wasn't even plowed the first few years we lived there. The path to the road, which was my only connection to the rest of the world (excluding the battery-operated radio with six bands my parents had given me), was maintained merely through use. By walking on it each day, I tramped the snow down into a usable track. This proved problematic in the spring when my winter path began to melt and I would crash through the crust innumerable times each trip I made across it.

It is said that shovelling snow is as strenuous as running at a pace of nine miles per hour. The average annual snowfall for Ottawa is about seven and a half feet. The snowfall increases considerably when one climbs from Ottawa north into the Gatineau Hills, where the average annual snowfall is closer to twelve feet. (The Canadian record annual snowfall was set in the winter of 1971–72 at Copeland, British Columbia — 80.3 feet!)

The work didn't go away with spring. Instead, other burdens presented themselves. When the road into the Farm was plowed, we could drive within easy walking distance of the cabin through the winter, but in the spring, when the thaw set in, certain patches of the dirt road turned to impassable mud. For anywhere from three to six weeks, we were forced to park our cars near where Montée Drouin met the highway, about a mile from my cabin. That meant, for that period of time, all my groceries (and anything else I needed) had to be carried in by hand. Needless to say, I didn't buy any two-fours of beer during mud season, and even a bottle of wine made one pause.

Spring also meant the preparation of the garden for planting as soon as the frost was gone from the earth. Removing the previous year's detritus, turning the soil, digging in the new compost, repairing fences, all to the encouraging appearance of the earliest spring shoots of asparagus and rhubarb. Later in spring came the actual planting. This meant cultivating rows to make the soil pliable, removing inevitable stones coughed up by winter's deep frost, making drills, and seeding. Seeding could prove an operation as fine and annoying as threading needles, especially when it came to the tiniest seeds such as those for carrots and radishes. One wanted to take special care because the effort put into careful hand-seeding meant less effort two or three weeks later when it came time to thin the young plants which, if thickly seeded, grew so close together it was almost impossible to separate them. There were also egg cartons and other boxes to be filled with soil and seeded for indoor starting of the more frost-sensitive plants. When the weather improved further, these could be put out into the garden and begin their outdoor cycles of fruiting and seeding.

Of course, this being the Gatineau Hills, tomatoes, beans, and other fragile plants in the garden required replanting after the inevitable late frost hit in the first week of June. It was an unusual summer that was long enough to ripen tomatoes fully. Most years we picked them green before the first heavy frost of September (or late August), and they had to finish their full-blown blush into redness on trays inside the house.

Finally, the garden is planted, no more snow falling, less wood to carry into the house because the weather has turned warm and none to split and pile until the fall. Summer has arrived. Time to relax.

Not yet. The new young plants have to be thinned soon after the seeds sprout and split the ground. Thinning of beans presents little difficulty, but thinning carrots and radishes is painful, back-breaking work in a large garden. Soon I notice that the upper part of the garden is looking a little dry. Lack of rain can be a disaster for young plants with shallow roots. Time to water. At the corner of the cabin stands a rain barrel, which fills each time a storm passes through or an all-day soak descends. I have tacked a board slant-wise on the roof to encourage the rainwater to run toward the corner below which the barrel sits. I use the water in the barrel to moisten the garden. I note with barely suppressed frustration

Part 8

that the full forty-five-gallon drum only waters the garden plants about one-quarter of an inch deep into the soil around them. Three days later, under a suddenly blistering sun, the garden is dry again. Since it hasn't rained, the barrel is empty. That means hauling water from the spring down the hill. The garden sucks it up the way a thirsty Irishman quaffs Guinness. After several hours of hauling, the garden is watered and the plants are safe, for the moment. If it doesn't rain in the following two or three days, and if the heat keeps up, I'll have to do it all over again.

The work seems endless. There is weeding to be done, and cultivating between the rows. And, suddenly, a bit of harvesting: a few meals of asparagus, a bounty of early radishes so hot they sear the backs of your eyeballs, or rhubarb so raw it requires a half pound of sugar for a single pie to be edible. Meanwhile, the chickens need feeding and the henhouse requires cleaning out before the hens die of methane poisoning, and the eggs have to be collected each morning.

Summer is the time to do any of the other necessary work around the house and farm. Replacing or cleaning windows, fixing sheds, ensuring all is right with the chimney. I didn't have a masonry chimney, so cleaning it involved taking apart all the cylindrical metal sections that comprised the chimney, hauling them outside and cleaning out the soot, then reassembling the entire works, making sure to replace any sections with holes or thin spots.

Finally, since it's hot and muggy, the outhouse reminds me it's time to empty it out because the hole underneath has filled up with you know what. The first four feet are rather raw and not a little disgusting, but after that I'm surprised to find that the lower sections have turned into soil. Eventually, it's done. A fine day's work, followed by an essential swim at a nearby lake, or at least a dip in the stream, which is always ice-cold no matter how hot the summer.

And, of course, the roof of the cabin needs re-shingling, but I think I'll leave that for the cool of autumn. In any case, it's time to make dinner, lunch, breakfast, to do the dishes, try to fix the car, trim the wicks on the lamps, or clean the globes, or fill the lamps with oil. Time to replace a screen that got torn, or take out the compost, or scythe the summer hay to keep a clear space around the cabin in a useless attempt to keep the bugs down, or to do whatever is next on the endless list that is life one day at a time.

Later in the summer, taking in the harvest involves a surprising amount of work, as well. Not just picking radishes, peas, beans, broccoli, cabbage, and carrots, but stringing the beans to dry them on the wall in front of the cabin (later to be soaked and used in soups and stews), shelling the peas, packing the tomatoes into newspaper. I even attempted to make sauerkraut one year with an abundance of cabbages from the garden. I followed the recipe with the attention to detail of a nuclear physicist or a French winemaker and brewed up a crock of rotten slop. Totally inedible. Another time I tried storing a small mountain of carrots in buckets filled with sand (I had heard this was a typical approach used by settlers), which I stashed under the cabin. Somehow, when it came time to harvest those carrots from their buckets a few months later, there was nothing left in them but moist sand. It was definitely trial and error when it came to life at the Farm.

And then it was autumn again. Time to start collecting and cutting firewood.

Part 9

I
Choices

THE QUESTION OF WHEN violence is or is not justified is an extremely complex one. William T. Vollmann recently published seven volumes (3,298 pages!), entitled *Rising Up and Rising Down*, on the subject — far be it from me to resolve the issue in a few spare paragraphs.

One view is that presented by Gandhi who said, quoting the *Dhammapada*: "Hatred does not cease by hatred at any time. Hatred ceases by love. This is an unalterable law." We can look at the world around us and see the truth that violence always leads to further violence. Hate leads to more hate. The question that arises is this: How does one apply Gandhi's view to situations in which violence is direct, overwhelming, and unresponsive to love.

In any discussion of pacifism and draft and war resistance, the chorus of dissenters can be heard loud and clear raising that age-old shibboleth: *What about Hitler*? What if you are dealing with an aggressor that seemingly has no conscience, meets love with violence and hate, and is unaffected by the power of public opinion? I have no idea what I personally would have done in the face of Hitler and National Socialism. Even in response to Hitler there was a considerable strain of pacifism in the United States. During the Second World War, 72,000 men applied for conscientious objector status. Of this number 27,000 ultimately failed their physicals and were exempted on that basis.

According to Vollmann, self-defence is the only case where use of violence is clearly justified. But where does "self-defence" begin? When someone comes at me or my family with a knife or gun? In distant Vietnam, because those in power believed the fall of Vietnam would lead to the communists ruling the world? In Iraq or Iran, because terrorists might get the bomb?

Vollmann uses the concept of imminence to further define self-defence — the attack one is defending oneself against must be imminent. But imminence can be defined in many ways and has been used over and over throughout history to justify the most egregious aggression and violence, to justify attacks on nations and peoples that, in sober reality, posed little threat at all. Vollmann goes into profound detail as he measures the calculus of violence, making fine distinctions among deterrence, retribution, and revenge, and when they are justified and not justified.

The ultimate problem, it seems, is that the definitions of all the terms used to describe and measure violence are coloured by the level of personal fear. Aggressors often feel war is "justified" by their need for deterrence because they fear "imminent harm." The need for deterrence always rises with the level of fear. It appears that the greater the fear, the more far-reaching is the perceived need for deterrence.

Ultimately, it seems that violence can only be defeated in the personal realm of the individual heart. It is where all violence begins. It can only be conquered at source. And it is apparent that violence begins with fear.

In March 2003 the Dalai Lama said: "Today, the world is so small and so interdependent that the concept of war has become anachronistic, an outmoded approach.... War ... should be relegated to the dustbin of history. Of course, the militaristic tradition may not end easily."

However, it is easy to convince people to go to war if you are first able to convince them that they have something to fear. The following appears in Gustave Gilbert's *Nuremberg Diary* and involves a conversation he had with Hermann Göring during the Nuremberg trials. Göring was chief of the Gestapo and second only to Hitler during the Nazi regime.

> "Why, of course, the people don't want war," Goering shrugged. "Why would some poor slob on a farm want to risk his life in a war when the best that he can get out of it is to come back to his farm in one piece. Naturally, the common people don't want war; neither in Russia nor in England nor in America, nor for that matter in Germany. That is understood. But, after all, it is the leaders of the country who determine the policy and

it is always a simple matter to drag the people along, whether it is a democracy or a fascist dictatorship or a Parliament or a Communist dictatorship."

"There is one difference," I [Gustave Gilbert] pointed out. "In a democracy the people have some say in the matter through their elected representatives, and in the United States only Congress can declare wars."

"Oh, that is all well and good, but, voice or no voice, the people can always be brought to the bidding of the leaders. That is easy. All you have to do is tell them they are being attacked and denounce the pacifists for lack of patriotism and exposing the country to danger. It works the same way in any country."

Peace is not something that will come from the top down. It cannot come from governments, or the United Nations, or religion, from political or social movements, or from anyone outside ourselves. It can only come from finding peace — the dissolution of fear — in each human heart. Peace on earth is intimately connected to peace of mind.

2
Wilderness

The wilderness is not just far away and dwindling, but implicit in things we use every day, as close at hand as a flat tire or a missed step.
— *Don McKay,* Vis à Vis, Field Notes on Poetry & Wilderness

WE WHO MOVED TO the Farm were part of the back-to-the-land movement, as it was called at the time. As a movement, it was informal and spontaneous, a sudden urge on the part of a significant number of people born between 1940 and 1955 in the cities and suburbs of the

Western world, in particular in North America, to move to the country to enjoy its peace and simplicity. It is estimated that as many as a million people were part of the back-to-the-land movement.

What prompted this strange exodus from the urban world? A reaction against politics and materialism was certainly part of it. Also, the fear of nuclear annihilation, which permeated the consciousness of the baby-boomer generation. When I was in elementary school in Cleveland, for example, the school used to hold air raid drills in case of nuclear attack. When the sirens sounded, the teachers instructed the children to hide under their desks. Even at age seven I had a fairly clear idea of what I was trying to hide from and the understanding that hiding under the desk would probably not help.

Getting back to the land was seen as a return to a semblance of sanity and the simple basic truths of life. The draw of the land itself also had something to do with this exodus — the profound security that land offers, the tranquility of the natural landscape. After the manic, engaged politics of the 1960s, there appeared to be a profound need for serenity.

The land is where our memories live, where our past has taken root. In *Landscape and Memory,* Simon Schama writes that "the rich loam of memory" is found just under the earth's surface. Our sense of survival and stability is tied to the land: along a river in Borisov or Cleveland; in the forests of Belarus or Canada; in the jungles of Vietnam or the rolling farmland of Ohio. We are figures in a landscape — our feet on a particular piece of the earth.

In the Americas the farmer became the keeper of the land — once it had been cleared of forest. The farmer became the embodiment of new myths, that is, the myths of a landscape tamed and ordered. The farmer was the tenant of the earth, responsible for guarding the seeds and ensuring that the annual cycle followed its normal path from planting to budding to fruiting and concluded again with the gathering of seeds.

The farmer was (and still is) responsible for maintaining the garden, the farm, which was considered an island of order in an ocean of dark and shadowy chaos. The farmer's duty involved keeping the chaos at bay so that mankind could live from the bounty of the earth. The farmer was to ensure fecundity and a natural order based on his understanding of the turning of the seasons, the tilling of soil, the domesticating and nurturing of animals, and the patterns of weather.

But, in northern Canada generally, and in northern Quebec in particular, the taming was never entirely established, for the wild, the chaotic, the unknown, could always re-establish its hegemony over the civilized world. There were many reasons for the continuing power of the wild in Canada and Quebec. The sheer length of winter in northern Canada was one — the farmer always lived at the edge of survival and, like Louis Drouin, often had to double as a lumberjack to make ends meet.

Another cause for the persistent power of the wild in Canada was the looming north itself. Head due north from the Farm and you might cross the occasional road, but essentially you found few humans for thousands of miles — endless bush, swamps, lakes, eventually tundra and the Arctic. The wildness, the emptiness, was always staring in the back door of the cabin — what Don McKay in *Vis à Vis* refers to as "the enormous, unnamable wilderness ... a wilderness we both long for and fear." (The Native peoples, of course, had a completely different relationship with the wilderness; after all, it was their ancestral land and they had always understood it in ways white culture could barely fathom.) For us the night out the back door of the cabin was a blank negative photo on which we could project anything — hope, fear, the unknown.

As Henry David Thoreau wrote in *The Maine Woods* (1846), "This was that Earth of which we have heard, made out of Chaos and Old Night. Here was no man's garden.... It was Matter, vast, terrific." Thoreau employs the archaic meaning of the word *terrific*, which is cognate with *terror*.

Vast, too is an intriguing word, for one of the characteristics of nature is that very vastness, that great emptiness that can swallow us up or make us realize our insignificance in terms of both space and time. Simon Schama writes of the "hero made minuscule by the mountain," an idea reflected in traditional Chinese landscape paintings in which the human figure is overwhelmed by mountains and rivers without end. I also picture Napoleon "cut down to size" as his imperial visions of conquest were overwhelmed by the vastness and enormity of a Russian winter and the Russian land. Nature itself swallowed up the Grand Army in the same way that American aspirations and delusions in Vietnam were swallowed by endless jungle, despite attempts to root it out with Agent Orange and napalm.

In speaking of the mid-nineteenth-century view of wilderness, Schama writes: "The presumption was that the wilderness was out there, somewhere, in the western heart of America, awaiting discovery, and that it would be the antidote for the poisons of industrial society." In Canada, in Quebec, the wilderness was right here. There was no need to "discover" it, no need to go west; it was all around you. In fact, the wild was always ready to devour you. You were forced to set your mind and your society against it simply in order to survive. For his collection of writings on Canada by foreign writers, the editor Greg Gatenby chose the appropriate title: *The Wild Is Always There*. The weather, the long winter, wild animals, clouds of insects, the vastness of the landscape — Canada appears to be tamed only along a horizontal line that extends a mere ninety miles north of the U.S./Canadian border. If Canada were a brain, it would have a thin layer of refined matter at the bottom of the brainpan, weighed down upon by a vast, empty landscape of natural chaos, the wild, wilderness.

Jean-Jacques Rousseau, the French philosopher, took a different view of wilderness. For Rousseau the wild was emblematic of freedom, or natural liberty, as represented by his noble savage who lived in harmony with nature. Cities, for Rousseau, were "the abyss of the human species," and the natural world and natural man were ideals destroyed by humankind's meddling. According to the Bible, Cain, the first murderer, was also the first human to build a city. In *A Short History of Myth*, Karen Armstrong states: "In the book of Genesis, the loss of the primordial paradisal state is experienced as a falling into agriculture."

But the world of the Farm included both — the tamed and the wild. There were cleared fields surrounded by hills of deep, shadowy forests and swamps. There was a road, but there could always be bears or wolves crossing that road. There were houses and gardens and apple trees, all of them surrounded by another, much larger world of wildness, shadow, and chaos. The landscape included both. How could it not?

To my mind, Louis embodied both worlds, as well: the civilized and the untamed. He was both a farmer and a lumberjack, with a nearly instinctual knowledge of crops, animals, the natural world, and the cycles of the seasons. But he was also an unpredictable drinker. When he was drunk, he was truly, absolutely drunk. And when he was sober, he was like a rock, immovable. He refused to run when a sergeant in the military told him to run. But, like any wise farmer, when the sun and moon said "plant," he planted, and when the seasons and the weather said "cut and harvest," he didn't hesitate or question but went straight ahead and cut and harvested.

When I moved to the Farm, the fields soon started to revert to their natural state of forest. Friends from more tamed lands such as southern Ontario or Ohio were aghast at the fact that I was allowing the fields to become overgrown and not keeping them trimmed back. Over the years the alder bushes began sprouting around the stream that cut through the heart of the field in front of the cabin and eventually they marched out across the field from there, like soldiers rising out of the earth. Alders are considered a scrub bush, not good for much of anything. But I knew they were just one stage in a cycle, in a turning of time that was larger than any of us humans passing through.

On one hand, it was true that the hard work of the first settlers in clearing the land was about to go to waste, so to speak. But aspens and evergreens would follow the alders, and then maples and other hardwoods as the field evolved through the natural cycle of a forest. I didn't think it was a horror for the field to return to wilderness, for the landscape to alter itself naturally. Both the tamed and the wild are essential, are necessary. Woodpeckers and chipmunks would live in that forest. Daisies and the wildflowers of the field would no longer bloom there, but other flowers would — trilliums and lady's slippers, as well as mushrooms and a myriad of other types of vegetation. The "savage" world would return because it had never really left. The Farm would become subsumed once again by the "wild."

The wild, the untamed, the chaos, is always closer than we realize. A somnolent river can suddenly flood, or catch fire, if we keep abusing it. Our fields and farms, our jungles, our land could be overrun by French soldiers, Russian soldiers, American soldiers. One morning we are pleasantly sowing seeds in the garden and before dark the same day the earth is being trampled by boots. The next day the nearby river could be swallowing those French soldiers, the jungle could be sucking young American troops into its tangle, the police could arrive at the door. The chaos always lives one step to the right or left. It's not far off. Flood, earthquake, bear attack, heart attack, incoming rockets, land mine, cancer.

Ultimately, the trees, the sky, the earth, and the animals are oblivious to our presence, our needs and desires. You could be a king or a corpse rotting into the ground and wilderness doesn't care. The wild, that is, nature, sends storms, earthquakes, life-giving sun, and crop-nurturing rain without any thought to its effect.

Nature has no opinion.

3
Pumpkin

I would rather sit on a pumpkin and have it all to myself than be crowded on a velvet cushion.

— *Henry David Thoreau,* Walden

HENRY DAVID THOREAU WAS one of the original back-to-the-landers, although the attractions of a rural life didn't go unnoted among the ancient Greeks and Romans. In *Walden, or Life in the Woods*, Thoreau wrote of his experiences living on Walden Pond in Massachusetts. "Nature is a wizard," Thoreau said, and it's hard to disagree when you've seen a loon shooting through limpid water twenty feet beneath the surface of a lake or the spangled dust of the Milky Way on a crisp winter night.

But Thoreau was also fully engaged with the politics of his day. He wrote against slavery and the war the United States was waging with Mexico in his essay *Civil Disobedience*, published in 1849. For Thoreau, to act according to individual conscience was not choice but a duty, a responsibility. He said: "Can there not be a government in which majorities do not virtually decide right and wrong, but conscience?" and "The only obligation which I have a right to assume is to do at any time what I think right." Since the mid-nineteenth century, he has been the poster boy for all conscience-driven individualists and those who maintain that the integrity of the natural world cannot be separated from the integrity of the person. Thoreau embodied two roles that would become hallmarks of the 1960s: the war resister and the back-to-the-lander.

In one sense, Thoreau was in a distinctly American vein. He was a freethinker and a loner, although it is said that he was, in fact, more sociable than his writings suggest. *Walden* reminds me strikingly of my early days as a near-hermit at the Farm. Like Thoreau, who "travelled a good deal" in the constrained limits of Concord, I "travelled a good deal" about the Farm, learning more and more about less and less, investigating a limited piece of the earth, a portion of landscape. To gaze, day after day, in all seasons, for years on end, at the same fields and hills and valleys, teaches one something that cannot be learned by driving at high speed through all the books in all the libraries in the world, nor can it be learned in a laboratory, or from looking out the crystalline window of a space capsule.

Thoreau didn't have much time for armies or for what he called an "undue respect for the law": "A common and natural result of an undue respect for law is, that you may see a file of soldiers, colonel, captain, corporal, privates, powder-monkeys, and all, marching in admirable order over hill and dale to the wars, against their wills, ay, against their common sense and consciences."

He added: "There will never be a really free and enlightened State until the State comes to recognize the individual as a higher and independent power, from which all its own power and authority are derived, and treats him accordingly." That, obviously, isn't a good recipe if you're interested in forming an army. Perhaps it is in their nature that the military and the freethinking, conscience-driven individual will forever be mutually exclusive.

4
Books: Kafka and Melville

I FIRST READ FRANZ Kafka's short stories at the Farm, sitting with my back against an apple tree in high summer. The tree was a third of the way up a hill at the edge of a field at the far northern end of the property. Each day I took a handful of books from the cabin and hiked for fifteen minutes down the dirt road to the apple tree where I spent three to four hours in the shade, reading, jotting, perhaps writing a poem. My view, to the west and south, encompassed a number of linked rolling fields, stands of pine and maple rising up and up in waves of green hills.

I read the Modern Library edition of Kafka, copyright 1936, which contained fifteen stories. "The Burrow" seemed particularly appropriate to my surroundings, as I often glimpsed groundhogs. ("But the most beautiful thing about my burrow is the stillness. Of course, that is deceitful. At any moment it may be shattered and then all will be over. For the time being, however, the silence is still with me.")

From my vantage point I saw hawks, as well, circling and tilting high in the blue. Perhaps it was the contrast that attracted me: that between Kafka's obsessive inner world, his claustrophobic "burrow," and the world that lay before me — open fields, empty sky, the rest of my life.

This end of the Farm was on the edge of wild Quebec bush country. If I had stood up from my comfortable seat at the base of the apple tree, turned around, and started walking north, I would have entered a wilderness that stretches to the Arctic. This was the area of the Farm where I had previously seen bears along a nearby stream, and I half hoped, half feared I would see another nearby. Various denizens of the insect world were my constant companions, especially ants, which I noted seemed to possess a dogged curiosity as they avidly explored the world at my feet.

Part 9

As I sat at the base of the apple tree, I balanced on the cusp between civilized and uncivilized realms, between the agricultural world and the world of untamed nature. In one direction, across the semi-cultivated fields, stood my cabin, the road out, the human world. In the other direction, up the hill behind me and over into the high swamp, pressed the wild, the untamed, the unknown. That comfortable seat on the earth was a gate between two worlds. A gate and a link, a threshold that connected apparently disparate things, the way the gate of a walled city or a door in a house marked both a connection and a separation.

The apple tree that served as my backrest had a strand of barbed wire passing right through it about three feet above the ground, the remains of an ancient fence long fallen into disuse. The apple tree had, with time, grown entirely around the wire obstruction. Somehow this seemed similar to the way a Kafka character would relate to the world. Or perhaps the tree stood for Kafka himself.

One winter, in the early years when I spent an inordinate amount of time alone, I read Herman Melville's *Moby-Dick* by coal-oil lamp at the kitchen table next to the pleasantly radiating wood stove, the fields outside deep with snow. Through long, near-silent evenings, I engaged with Melville's tale, exploring the symbolism and meaning of the colour white as well as Ahab's obsessive hunt for the great white whale, Moby-Dick.

For Melville the white whale represented the immensity and inscrutability of the non-human universe, a world with which we have no means to communicate and little ability to understand. The untamed world, wild and uncivilized, that constantly stood outside my back door was the great incomprehensible north leaning against the back wall of the cabin. In a sense, that untamed world was leaning against the back door of Canada itself.

By the light of my lonely lamp, I sat and read *Moby-Dick* in that wintry place, on the cusp between worlds, on the threshold of my life, as it was and as it would be.

When one lives a winter in a log cabin in Quebec with no electricity and no running water, with overnight snowfalls of one to two feet not uncommon, with the trees in the swamp out back snapping and cracking in the bitter January cold, with the endlessness and timelessness of it all, the deep white days and the deep black nights, one grows obsessed with winter.

Winter, I discovered, was my white whale.

Part 10

I
Commune

DURING THE VIETNAM ERA, draft resistance and desertion were one way for young people to make a statement; going back to the land was another. Between 1965 and 1973, it is estimated that 2,000 communes, most of them rural, were established in the United States with approximately 250,000 members, by far the largest communal movement ever attempted in North America (although putting a number on the 1960s phenomenon is extremely difficult — one key element of communes was that they were a movable feast, always shrinking and expanding as people came and went).

Communes have a long history, likely starting with the Essenes, who founded the first utopian-style communes in the Middle East during the time of Christ. The Essenes lived communally, sharing all goods, and practised asceticism at a time when the Romans were the power in the region.

In the Middle Ages the term *communes* referred to small cities in northern Italy in which people expressed their desire to be free and tax themselves, in direct opposition to outside rulers such as the Holy Roman emperor or the pope. *Commune* was later used by Paris malcontents in 1871 who opposed the national government at Versailles and established their own administration in the city. The Commune of Paris was ruthlessly suppressed by French soldiers who left behind 33,000 dead, the streets so slick with blood that horses kept slipping and falling.

The Chinese established the world's most complete commune system during the reign of Mao Zedong. Beginning in 1958, 700 million people were placed into 26,578 communes in what was called the Great Leap Forward. Mao's attempt to modernize both industry and agriculture was an abysmal failure. The individual's life was controlled in every possible way from cradle to grave. No one owned anything, everyone worked for the commune, and the elderly lived in "houses of happiness." Loudspeakers over the fields reminded the people of how lucky they were and what a great thing they were doing.

Certainly, this idea of a commune was not at all what we were trying to do, in our own small way, at the Farm. Mao's vision was in complete opposition to the ideal world of the individual posited by someone like Thoreau. And I don't think a farmer/lumberjack like Louis Drouin would have lasted long in that world. Either he would have been obliterated or he would have thrown a chain around Mao's China and pulled it down with his two strong workhorses.

The Great Leap Forward was an astonishing disaster and tragedy. An estimated twenty million people died of starvation or diseases related to starvation between 1959 and 1962.

The United States, too, has been the site of numerous attempts to build communes, many based on religious values and others that were secular. The Shakers (major producers of opium in their day) and the Hutterites are well known, but there were hundreds of other attempts to establish communes. The United States, since the days of William Penn, had always been seen as a nation of religious tolerance and cheap land. The Hutterites, just one of many religious communes, came to the United States in 1874 and started with a few hundred members. Hutterites had lived communally in Central Europe since the sixteenth century. Today, 40,000 Hutterites still live in over 400 colonies.

Perhaps the strangest communal effort of the nineteenth century in the United States was that founded by Cyrus R. Teed in the 1880s. Like many another religious crackpot before and since, Teed, a medical doctor, considered himself the New Messiah. He established the Koreshan Unity and started a commune in Florida, which eventually gained 4,000 members. Their primary belief? The earth is a hollow sphere and we live inside it.

Toward the end of the nineteenth century, interest in communes fell off considerably, partly due to the attractions of a new theory of politics, society, and economies. Socialism and communism proved of significant interest to many people who would otherwise likely have been drawn to communal life. Although communes in the 1960s and 1970s were founded for a wide range of reasons, certainly a lack of confidence in the ability of traditional political, or Marxist and other radical politics, to solve the world's problems was one major factor.

Traditionally, many of the communes across the United States, both secular and religious, had a utopian bent. Their founders hoped to establish heaven on earth. Certainly, the young people of the back-to-the-land movement began with stars in their eyes, but it didn't take long to come down to earth. A single planting season would prove the incredible effort required to live off the land, and a single winter in Quebec (or any other part of Canada and most of the northern states) would weed out a significant number of wannabes.

In any case, the disaffected always seem to head for the hills where the reach of the government will tend to be less intrusive. Alternatively, the urban disaffected seek refuge in the concrete webs at the heart of the largest cities, as did tens of thousands of black draft resisters during the Vietnam War.

Ultimately, the rural commune of the 1960s was both a reaction to the status quo and a loosely held ideology that manifested in a variety of ways. Back-to-the-land hippies were reacting against mainstream society, life in the suburbs, degraded politics, rampant consumerism, and meaningless labour.

In a sense, hippiedom was an anti-ideology. It mixed anti-government protest with anti-materialism, a belief in simplicity and freedom of expression. One key element was opposition to a world where nuclear catastrophe was a constant threat. There was an interest in alternate lifestyles, which manifested itself in the well-known clichés of hippiedom: long hair, scruffy beards, tie-dyed T-shirts, bell-bottoms, torn jeans, sandals, and the embracing of poverty.

Hippies tried their best not to take regular jobs, preferring self-employment, especially in trades such as carpentry or in the crafts. Music pervaded everywhere. Rock and roll was embraced. The latest song by The Beatles, The Rolling Stones, Bob Dylan, Jimi Hendrix, Joni Mitchell, or Pink Floyd became the latest hippie anthem. Experimentation in drugs and mystical spiritual approaches, especially eastern, were common. Vegetarianism and macrobiotics were another area of exploration. Brown rice became a staple.

Mainstream journalists wrote that "hedonism" was the ideology of the hippie commune. The media were mainly interested in sex and drugs on communes, and these often became the focus of reports and stories on the hippies and the commune movement. This view is simplistic in the extreme and says more about the media and what sells than it ever did about the hippies.

Part of the wholesale rejection of mainstream society was certainly the rejection of its mores, especially as they related to sex. The changing times brought change right across the board in every aspect of life. The prevailing attitude of free love was that restrictions on sexual behaviour should be abolished or simply ignored.

It cannot be said that hippies invented anything entirely new. From 1848 until 1879, to take but one example, the Oneida community in the United States practised its own version of a biblically based free love, called Complex Marriage, in which, as Constance Noyes Robertson writes in *Oneida Community: An Autobiography 1851–1876*, quoting her founder father, John Humphrey Noyes, "The new commandment is that we love one another, and that not by pairs, as in the world, but en masse." Nevertheless, there was little historical precedent for the kind of flowering of sexuality, freedom of choice, openness to homosexuality and lesbianism, and the upsurge of feminist power that followed in the wake of the hippie movement.

Nudity was certainly an essential feature of our lives at the Farm but, obviously, due to the cold and the bugs, nudity in the bush country of Quebec, and much of Canada in general, is restricted to a few weeks in the summer, sometimes as much as six or eight weeks in an unusually warm year. We often went to a lonely lake in Gatineau Park to skinny-dip, afterward sitting around shamelessly, men and women, sometimes kids, in the altogether without the least embarrassment.

Nudity was standard procedure for our group saunas, as well. Nudity felt natural, and the human body was nothing to be ashamed of. Of course, we were all in our twenties and in good shape.

As far as sex goes, though, we never really discussed it. Everyone wanted to partner up as soon as possible, although there was almost no sharing of partners and no attempts at group marriage at the Farm. We must have been the straightest, dullest commune on the face of the planet if the articles in *Life* and *Time* were to be believed.

2

Immigrant

WHEN I FIRST MOVED to Canada in the summer of 1970, I knew that I had to apply for landed immigrant status if I wanted to remain in the country and be able to work. The granting of landed immigrant status was based on a point system that had recently been established by the Canadian government. An applicant received points for being under a certain age, points for years of education, points for skills and training, and so on. I learned that a job offer in Canada was a requirement, as well.

As I had no easy means to land a job in Canada, I was able to convince my father to request a job offer from an associate of his who was the general manager of his company's branch plant in Toronto. I had worked for Curtis Industries in Cleveland (where my father was a vice-president) for several summers while in university. What I recall most vividly from those summers is waiting for hours in the family car in the company parking lot long after I had finished my day and while my father worked late. I read huge volumes of poetry as I sat patiently in the big Buick LeSabre, including Donald Allen's collection of the Beat poets and others in *The New American Poetry*, which introduced me to Allen Ginsberg, Jack Kerouac, Gregory Corso, Frank O'Hara, and many other poets of the 1950s. Waiting in a car was never so much fun: "Got up and dressed up / and went out & got laid" (Jack Kerouac, 113th Chorus, *Mexico City Blues*). My introduction to the Beats inspired me to write a truckload of sophomoric poetry that summer. I was hooked.

The letter with the job offer, which my father had arranged, came on stationery from Curtis Industries in Rexdale, Ontario, and is dated June 30, 1970. It reads:

Dear Mr. Frutkin:

This is to advise you that your application for employment has been approved.

You are to report for work on July 15, 1970 at 8 o'clock A.M.

You are to be assigned to the position of Supervisor, Shipping and Receiving, at a salary of $100.00 per week. Fringe benefits will be as discussed.

I will be looking forward to your arrival.

Yours truly,
B.L. Burnside
General Manager

Across the bottom of the sheet the letter reads: "Automotive & Industrial Parts & Fasteners * Keys & Key Machines * Hardware Specialties." Nothing about having to be acquainted with the Beat poets.

On July 15, 1970, job offer in hand, I headed from Quebec to the American border near Cornwall, Ontario. I was travelling in a van with American friends who were living in the village of Wakefield near the Farm, a young married couple who were also seeking landed immigrant status that day. Roger wasn't a draft resister — he had a deferment owing to a lifelong epilepsy affliction. Little did we know that I would be returning to Quebec alone.

In mid-afternoon we crossed the border and entered the United States. Several miles down the highway we turned around and promptly drove back, exiting the United States. We pulled up to the squat, official-looking customs building at the Canadian border, parked, and entered. At the desk we announced that we wanted to request landed immigrant status. We were referred to an official, who ushered me into his office, while Roger and Sylvia waited their turn.

The grey, bitter-looking, Canadian customs man didn't appear to be pleased to accept any hippies into his office, let alone his country. I sat down in front of his desk and he proceeded to ask me questions from the official list before him, totalling my points as we went along. I raised a silent prayer to heaven in thanks that he was forced to follow a point system that allowed him little leeway in deciding whether to accept or reject applicants. His unsmiling face asked, "Age?"

"Twenty-two," I said.

He jotted down a figure unseen by me. "Level of education?"

"B.A.," I said, handing him my certificate.

He inspected the certificate with the eyes of a lizard watching a fly float by, then gave it back. Again he jotted down a figure. I swallowed hard. He glanced up and, without looking at me, asked, "Do you have an offer of employment in Canada?"

"Yes." I handed him the letter.

He inspected the piece of paper, then jotted down more notes. "Amount of money you are bringing into Canada?"

"One hundred and ten dollars."

He marked this down. "Amount you will transfer at a later date?"

"Two thousand eight hundred and ten dollars."

I handed him my bank book as proof. He studied it, snapped it shut, and held it out for me while staring at the sheet before him. His face was a mask, revealing nothing of the simple column of numbers that would determine my fate.

The customs officer paused, considered the form before him, and added up the figures. "Welcome to Canada," he said in an entirely flat voice with no hint of welcome in it. He didn't offer his hand.

I exited the office and waited in a plastic chair while my friends were interviewed as a couple. They seemed to be taking a long time, much longer than I had. I started to wonder what was happening. Finally, an hour later they came out of the office, bleak looks on their faces. The little bureaucrat hadn't altered his expression one bit as he strode out behind them, went to the counter, stamped several official papers as if he were tenderizing a slab of veal, handed the sheets to them, turned around, and disappeared back into his office, closing the door behind.

I raised a questioning look to Roger and Sylvia. Roger couldn't speak, so Sylvia spoke for him. "They refused him entry because of his epilepsy."

"What? I thought he had a letter from a doctor that it was under control with medication. How can they do that?"

Roger was moving from stunned to angry. "The letter didn't matter one bit. We've been arguing with him for an hour. The guy's a real prick."

Sylvia glanced around. "We have to go back to the States. We can't even drive you back. You'll have to find your own way."

We said our farewells, they got into their van and drove into New York State, and I strolled down the highway, hitchhiked into Cornwall (which reeked from the local pulp mill), stayed at a cheap hotel that night where I checked in without a single piece of luggage, had a fitful night's sleep, and took a bus the next day back to Ottawa.

Four and a half months later I received a letter from the Canadian Department of Manpower and Immigration dated December 4, 1970. It read:

> Dear Sir:
>
> This refers to your application for permanent admission to Canada.
>   I am pleased to inform you that you have been granted the status of "Landed Immigrant" effective 4 December 1970.
>   The attached Canadian Immigration Identification Card is an important document which should be retained as evidence of your immigration status.
>
> Yours very truly,
> W.D. McNaughton,
> Officer-in-Charge

Attached to the letter was a photocopy of a form called Canadian Immigrant's Record Card, which included the answers I had given to questions at the Cornwall border crossing, such as whether or not I or anyone in my family had suffered from mental illness or tuberculosis, or been convicted of a criminal offence, or been refused admission or deported from Canada. Nothing about epilepsy. Under Box 22, Medical Category, a single word was typed: "Passed."

In Box 10, Intended Occupation, it read: "Supervisor, Stock." I never made it to Rexdale, though, despite the wishes of my parents that I take the job there at Curtis Industries. I had other plans, so I was willing to forgo the $100 a week I was offered. The bush, as we call it in Canada, beckoned.

3
Christmas, Duck

An autumn night at the cabin. It was always a small shock to hear a knock at the door out in the middle of nowhere. I opened the door and there stood Vietnam vet Jim with what appeared to be a full-grown white duck in his arms. They were both smiling.

"What's that?" I said.

"A duck," Jim said as he stepped inside. "His name is Christmas, because that's the idea."

"Oh?"

"We fatten him up for the next couple of months and then have him for Christmas dinner."

"Quack!" said Christmas, looking unworried.

"Where did you get him?"

Jim put the duck on the floor and shook his steel Montagnard bracelet from Vietnam down his wrist. The duck waddled around, investigating the cabin, immediately found the cat dish, and gobbled the few bits of dry cat food left in it.

"I got drunk at the Wakefield Inn and was walking past a yard and saw this duck right by the fence, so I leaned over the fence and snatched it up."

"Probably some kid's pet."

Jim shrugged, still half in the bag. He sat down at the kitchen table.

"What's for dinner?"

"Bean stew," I said. "What else?"

Christmas survived Christmas, and New Year's, as well. The first rule of animal husbandry is to avoid naming one's edibles. Christmas the holiday came and went and Christmas the duck was now a full-fledged pet, with his own little fenced yard near the garden and a steady supply of leftovers to nosh.

Sometime after Christmas, the holiday, I decided to move into Wakefield for a month or two to take over Wally's job as night janitor at the Wakefield Inn while he returned to the United States for an extended visit. I rented a house along the highway into the village for two months.

Moving day came and I loaded up my VW bug with the necessary goods for dressing, cleaning myself, cooking, and sleeping. The last thing I threw into the car was my cat and Christmas, the duck. Christmas, I noticed, had grown rather off-white with his lack of a swimming hole. Worse than off-white — he was filthy. He sat quietly in the back seat while I drove.

After I got to my tiny new bungalow, I unpacked and ran a full, deep bath for Christmas in the bathroom. When I placed him in the tub, I don't think I've ever seen a happier bird. He immediately started flapping his wings and dipping his head underwater.

Meanwhile, I unloaded the rest of the car and arranged things for my new life. An hour later I returned to the bathroom to find the tub empty of water and Christmas the duck absolutely pure white. The rest of the bathroom was soaked and dripping from ceiling to floor.

For the rest of my stay in Wakefield, Christmas lived in a shed behind the house where I kept him well fed on stale bread from Ormes Bakery down the road on the far side of the village. Ormes was where the village drunk, Loren Brown, slept on cold nights, his body pressed against the outside of the bakery's fireplace.

Loren was a character out of a Charles Dickens novel. A shambling, hunched-over fellow, stocky, always dressed in shabby clothes, he sometimes slept in abandoned cars and could always be found in the Wakefield Inn when he had an extra quarter to spend on a draft beer. He was a gentle soul, never bothered anyone, and always had a wide smile

Part 10

on his face despite his difficult circumstances

The Wakefield Inn was one of those old-style taverns that still existed at the time in Ontario and Quebec. One side, the one with the lone pool table, was for MEN ONLY, as it said on the sign over the entrance. The other side, with dining tables and carpeting, was for LADIES AND ESCORTS.

On a late Friday afternoon I was having a beer with some friends on the men only side. The room was packed with workers and local farmers celebrating the end of the week. Loren was sitting alone, quietly drunk on the day's bottle of rotgut he had downed earlier, nursing his beer. Into the bar spilled some of the tougher residents of Wakefield, in particular one fellow whose name seemed utterly appropriate for his role in this little drama of village life. Dalton Black ran a service station just outside of town along the highway. The rumour was that he had been fired from the Ottawa police force for killing a man in questionable circumstances, and one look at his craggy face told people this wasn't a guy to be messed with, whether the rumour was true or not. Black, strangely enough, always dressed in black, and this day he was true to form. But there was one accouterment that didn't fit the mould. Square-shouldered and thick-haired, Black was carrying a fresh, long-stemmed white rose in his right hand.

The ex-cop entered the tavern, glanced around the bar, walked straight up to Loren Brown (the whole room of drinking men turning to stare at this bit of live theatre), and pulled open Loren's tattered and stained sport coat. As Loren looked up in stupefied shock, Black shoved the flower down inside. "There you go, Lornie," he said, smiling mockingly, patting the coat shut, and turning on his heel to join his cronies at another table.

Loren gazed straight ahead, drunkenly stunned, the head of the white rose bobbling out of his coat.

After three weeks, I tired of mopping up vomit in the washrooms every Friday and Saturday night at the Wakefield Inn and quit my job, heading back to the Farm in late winter, Christmas the duck in tow.

A few months later Christmas disappeared from his pen one night for good, probably snatched by a fox or a raccoon. Some wild animal living at the Farm had his holiday feast a little late that year.

4
Wakefield

I LIVED IN WAKEFIELD several times for short periods during those years. It was the closest large village to the Farm, with a gorgeous natural setting on a wide, lazy bend in the Gatineau River. A short way upriver was a series of corrugated rapids and a historic wooden covered bridge. The seventy-year-old bridge was burned down in an act of mindless vandalism in 1984 when someone soaked a car in gasoline in the middle of the span and set it on fire. Through considerable community effort a replacement for the old bridge was opened twelve years later.

In the 1970s, Wakefield was an intriguing combination of the hip and the traditional. A few middle-aged gay couples and recently arrived hippies lived there, along with an entire choir of old-time churchgoers. The regional hospital, located in Wakefield, was founded by a pioneering doctor named Harold Geggie, whose life story is a fascinating, heartbreaking tale of midnight rides on horse-drawn sleds through deep winter snows to attend children dying of typhus on surrounding farms among the hills. He had three sons, all doctors, all of whom worked at the hospital. In an imagined scene out of a Marx Brothers movie, I always pictured the loudspeaker in the hospital booming, "Calling Dr. Geggie, Dr. Geggie, and Dr. Geggie."

The MacLaren family had been the long-time lumber barons of the area, and their grand house still stands in Wakefield, overlooking the waterfall on La Pêche River and the old flour mill, which is now a fancy country hotel and spa. Back when I lived at the Farm, the huge MacLaren house served as the Wakefield Library, a dark and dingy resting place for a quantity of dusty books.

The last of the MacLaren line was an ancient dowager who had been relegated to a cramped apartment above the post office in the village and was busily drinking down the remains of the family fortune. One day she invited Jochen, Fritz, and me up to her apartment for a drink after meeting us in the post office downstairs. A fascinating old woman, she asked us endless slurred, though intelligent, questions about why these two Germans had come here and what hippies wanted from life. Her preferred poison was gin, and she downed three gin and tonics to our one as she emptied the bottle and started on another. It wasn't quite 11:00 a.m.

Up a dirt road behind the MacLaren house, in a high field overlooking the surrounding hills, one comes to the MacLaren Cemetery. Here Lester B. Pearson is buried in an unpretentious grave, along with several hundred former residents of Wakefield, almost all Anglos. I found one French name the day I visited: Vaillancourt. Lots of Browns, McNairs, MacLarens, and Kennedys. When one considers the lack of Anglo names in the Wolf Lake cemetery, it is clear that Canada's two solitudes transcend this life.

Lester Pearson is still the only Canadian to have received the Nobel Peace Prize, for his work during the Suez Crisis in 1957, six years before his election as prime minister of Canada. His placement in this quiet graveyard and the low-key treatment given his remains is a testament to the way in which Canadians tend to deal with politicians and fame. There are no signs in the village to indicate the site, no signs on the dirt road that climbs up from the waterfall and the mill. There are no kiosks selling photos of Pearson or copies of books he wrote or even any requests for donations for the upkeep of his grave. There is only a Canadian flag, a small plaque, and his headstone, not standing alone but mixed in with the others. Nothing more. It is a beautiful spot, high above the village, overlooking the surrounding hills. Not beautiful in a Rocky Mountains majestic way, but in a quiet, modulated, soft, and subtle Gatineau Hills way. If you didn't know the grave of a former prime minister was there, you could easily miss it, which makes it that much more enjoyable to come across by accident.

My only other run-in with a politician in Wakefield happened the winter when I was living there. I had just come down into the village from an afternoon of cross-country skiing through the snowbound fields nearby. I removed my skis and went into an old-time grocery store owned by a local character named Karl Cross. It wasn't old-time in any kind of pretentious sense — it really was just an old store with wooden floors, high wooden shelves stacked with labelled jars of herbs and canned goods, and counters of dark wood and thick glass. It was nearing dusk, which in the Gatineaus in winter meant it was probably coming on four in the afternoon. I asked

Karl for a pound of cheese, which he proceeded to cut from a wagon wheel of cheddar on the counter. He placed the piece of cheese on a sheet of waxed brown paper, which he folded, tying it with twine that he pulled from a roll that hung on a trapeze-like bar above his head.

As Karl was slightly bent over, attending to my purchase, the bell on the front door tinkled and another customer entered. Karl glanced up, peering over his bifocals, and said under his breath, "Ah, here he comes, mad as a hatter."

I turned and looked. It was Tommy Douglas, the long-time federal MP from Saskatchewan and one of the founders of the New Democratic Party. He is considered the father of universal public health care in Canada and happens to be the grandfather of actor Kiefer Sutherland. Born in 1904, he must have been in his late sixties when I saw him entering Karl Cross's store. In 2004 he would be voted the Greatest Canadian of All Time in a nationwide CBC Television contest. Apparently, he had a cottage somewhere in the vicinity of Wakefield. Maybe, that day, he needed cheese, too, and perhaps he really was mad as a hatter. Wakefield was that kind of place. Canada was that kind of place. There was no undue reverence accorded to fame.

5
Earth

Louis Drouin seemed incapable of speaking in a normal voice. His voice either boomed out from his barrel chest as if he were shouting orders to his apparently half-deaf workhorses, or he remained immersed in a silence as deep as the forest. It's hard to say if there was any thinking going on inside that silence. If there was, it was the slow, heavy thinking of a bear or a bull or one of his massive horses. The mechanism of his thinking turned over at the pace of a cartwheel rather than a car wheel. It was a thinking slowed by the ice and frigidity of winter or stuck in the mud of spring — a thinking weighted by the clods and endless sweaty labour of summer or the heft of a thousand logs of autumn. It was a fire that burned without leaping, strong and steady, without flash, without show.

Louis was a peasant through and through. The word *peasant* is cognate with *pagan*, from the Latin *pagus*, a village or rural district. Originally, the word referred to a boundary post and meant "to fix firmly in the earth." The suggestion of boundary speaks again to the typically constrained world of the peasant and his ties to the land.

We usually think that this type of limited view leads to narrowness of mind and ignorance, but that small space, bounded by fences and surrounded by forest, could have infinite depth to make up for its lack of breadth. In fact, the knowledge that Louis had of the earth, the seasons, weather, horses, pigs, potatoes, and other crops, of trees and lumbering tools, must have been deeply rooted. He was "fixed firmly in the earth," as was any farmer, as have been all farmers for thousands of years. I picture him standing in a recently plowed field. He bends down and picks up a handful of soil and stares at it — and *knows*. He knows what it is, how it will behave, what will grow in it, and what will fail to grow. The earth speaks to him. He smells the soil in his palm and understands further what this earth is made of, without recourse to chemical names and analyses, without knowledge of nitrogen and potassium. If the soil smells sweet, and the weather co-operates, there will be enough potatoes to last until next spring.

Curiously, the word *farm* also connects to the idea of "firmness." *Farm* is cognate with *firm* and, oddly, *firmament*. The root of *farm* goes back to Middle French *fermer*, "to make a firm agreement or a contract," and the Latin *firmus*, "solid, strong." It also has a fascinating connection to the Italian *firma*, which means "signature." Perhaps that is one reason why Louis's mark, the *X* that he made on the Farm contract so long ago, had such a memorable effect on me.

The connection of the word *farm* to the word *firmament*, meanwhile, is truly intriguing. The Late Latin *firmamentum* means "firmness." The etymologists aver that this suggests authority (apparently from above) and thus from the sky itself. Of course, agriculture, cities, and written language also brought monotheism, and turned the gods of field and forest into the God of Heaven. Perhaps the classical view that the sky was actually a solid arch or vault helps make the etymological connection more viable.

In any case, I find it fitting that, when I stand in the field at night and gaze up at the stars, there exist connections in language itself between heaven and earth, between the Farm and the firmament, between the land and Louis's signature on a contract.

How odd it must have seemed to Louis and other local farmers to see us arrive on the land and attempt to grow crops. We were starting from scratch, our learning from books and our own observations. It was certainly the temper of the times that we had to do things our own way, even if it was the wrong way. This was true of farming, and it was also true of our legal relationship at the Farm. We tried to learn to farm, and some of us became spectacular failures at it, although most of us became at least competent gardeners. We also took our own approach to the law, and the results were predictably chaotic.

A formal legal contract existed for the Farm, as I pointed out earlier, a paper that had been passed along the generations. But since we considered ourselves a new type of settler, we felt we required a new type of contract to help define aspects of our relationship among ourselves and with the land. So we wrote up our own agreement and soon realized that this was just one more way in which our world and the greater world meshed uncomfortably, if they meshed at all.

It only seemed natural that we needed a contract to define what should be done or "forborne" by the parties to that contract. We titled our first contract "Deed of Ownership/Partnership" or simply "Farm Contract." I wrote it up after discussions with the various residents at that time. I then sent it to my oldest brother, Bud, and his wife Ann, who were living in New Haven, Connecticut, and were the majority owners of the property. They made a few corrections and deletions and promptly returned it.

As these things go, the contract was a model of economy and straightforwardness. I don't think William Penn himself could have drafted a document more sensible and appropriate. Unfortunately, it was a product of its laissez-faire times and didn't mesh easily with the realities and arcane complexities of the law. It consisted of two pages only. The first page stated the names of the owners (thirteen of them on this first contract) and the number of shares each person, or couple, owned. The number of total shares was

190, equivalent to the number of total acres of the Farm (Paul and Colleen had severed ten acres from the original 200-acre farm when they built their house). Thus my brother Bud, and his wife, Ann, owned sixty-four shares and I owned forty-six. All the others listed, singles and couples, owned at least ten shares each, which was the minimum holding we allowed.

The second page was titled "Restrictions" and consisted of eight points. The first of these stated: "the land will be developed for purposes of recreation, light farming, and cottage industries." This was required because we didn't want the owners, or anyone else, to strip the land of its trees or to start digging for gold or uranium. Only later would we learn that we had absolutely no control over this. All mineral rights, surface and sub-surface, belong to the government, which is always ready and willing to lease them to mining companies. At this writing, unfortunately, the Farm has already been staked by a Canadian uranium mining company.

Other points dealt with types of buildings allowed (single-family dwellings), how to sell shares (right of first refusal for present owners), admittance of new owners, how to vote on major questions, and so on. An attempt to delineate what would happen upon the death of an owner or owners was removed as we learned this could only be covered by a personal will.

Meetings dealing with the contract and other business aspects of the Farm were gruelling. No one enjoyed them. All who took part would use them as an opportunity to vent endless frustrations, unearth bitter feelings, and air resentments, and eventually the meetings stopped happening altogether. Some later owners, who had originally entered into the agreement, eventually sold to outsiders, who hadn't been voted in according to the agreement, and a tangled legal mess ensued.

One time I decided to take the document to our notary in Hull, where I had signed the original deed of sale with Louis. I wanted to straighten everything out, to see if we couldn't somehow notarize or legalize the agreement we had all discussed and signed in good faith on entering into the Farm. The notary — he was always extremely elegant in his dress and manners — looked at the document with what can only be called a thinly disguised distaste at its apparent attempt to circumvent the usual approach to legal affairs.

He shrugged and shook his head. "This all appears to be very complicated. I don't really understand why you feel the need to have this. What did you want me to do?"

I explained again. The expression on his face resembled someone watching a television show in a language he didn't speak.

Either he didn't want to dirty his hands with a situation so extra-legal and primitive, or he truly didn't know what to make of us.

I left the office frustrated, my questions unanswered (perhaps I didn't know the right questions to ask — always a difficulty when dealing with legal matters). My attempt to clarify the Farm's legal relationship was a total failure and my pockets significantly lighter.

6

Spring

No evil word she spoke
Nor never told a lie.
And now she reigns in heaven above
With angels in the sky.

ON THE FIRST GORGEOUS day of spring, the sky blue and soft, I'm staring down at a poem on the grave of Jane Link who died on June 28, 1857, "Aged 3 yrs. & 8 mos." Unlike some of the other graves here, hers doesn't have a small footstone to accompany the headstone. Fiddleheads and yellow flowers sprout from the grass of numerous graves in the Old Chelsea Protestant Cemetery in western Quebec about a half-hour north of Ottawa and a half-hour south of the Farm. Some of the headstones are blank, worn by time and weather, the combination of rain, snow, sun, wind, and years colluding to take memory back all the way to nothingness. On others the story still visible is heartbreaking: Philip and Mary Lippard, for example, had children die at the ages of eight, two, three, five, and six months. The cemetery is filled with the graves of children, testament to the harshness of life in the Gatineau Hills in the nineteenth century.

The most famous personage buried here is Asa Meech, who died in 1849 at seventy-four years. He is considered the first important settler of the Gatineaus, having come here from Massachusetts. A ragged crack, a thin wavering line, cuts diagonally across his gravestone, splitting it nearly in two. That split, that accidental division in granite, seems somehow freighted with meaning. Nearby Meech Lake in Gatineau Park (site of the failed Meech Lake Accord) was named after him.

In a newer part of the cemetery I come across, quite by accident, the grave of my first wife's father, whose burial I attended in 1977, but whose exact location I had forgotten. He died at age fifty-eight and seemed like an old man at the time.

A short while later I enter Gatineau Park and begin my planned hike in the spring woods. As I walk up a trail in the valley below the hills, I notice the first green lace of spring buds topping the trees on the heights against the blue sky.

If conditions are right (and they aren't right every year), you may have a week of fine spring weather in the Gatineaus in early May when the snow is entirely gone, it's not raining, and the air has warmed sufficiently to walk in the forest in shirt sleeves before the blackflies and mosquitoes hatch from their eggs and take over this world. Spring is short here, short and intense.

As I walk I notice that the crowns of the hardwoods are just starting to unfurl their green buds, the forest floor is a smooth carpet of last year's fallen leaves, and the boles of the trees can be seen clearly at eye level with no interfering brush. The forest is so wide-open, you can discern the raw outline of the hills (as if a living contour map), the shape of every erratic, and the exposed crumbling bedrock characteristic of the region. The forest looks like a well-tended park in England before the wild again begins to take over with its chaos of scrubby brush growing to eye level and its voracious, ubiquitous insects. But, for now, each white birch within a thousand feet can be clearly discerned, and the tiny yellow flowers and white blossoms along the trail are drinking down their moment of light while they can.

Throughout the forest, and not just along the path where most of the other flowers gather, the elegant, lily-like white trilliums are starting to swirl open while the smaller maroon trilliums, their velvet texture like moth wings, have blossomed a day or two earlier. The trail is edged with bright yellow coltsfoot of the aster family as well as tiny yellow trout lilies, also known as dogtooth violets. The distinctive speckled leaves of the trout lily suggest the mottled skin of a trout, or light passing through the water of a stream.

The forest floor is also blooming with inch-wide white bloodroot flowers of the poppy family. The bright reddish-orange juice of the stem is toxic and has been used to treat skin cancers and warts, and is employed commercially in toothpaste and mouthwash. There are also several types of flowers in the purslane family, tiny beautiful white blossoms with delicate purple veins. And, finally, I find a single plant of squirrel corn with white and pink orchid-like blossoms reminiscent of the better known, aptly named Dutchman's breeches (they resemble a pair of baggy breech-length pants).

In a week or so the forest will be transformed into a wild frenzy of green, and hordes of flying creatures hungry for blood will carry you away piece by piece. Any human without good reason to be here will stay out.

My walk is finished and I head home. Before starting the car I sit for a moment and recall the split in the Asa Meech gravestone. I contemplate the thin line between things: the line between two cultures and languages, between a quiet graveyard and irresistible spring, between those who can enjoy the birdsong in the high trees and those immersed in silence forever.

7
War Museum

IN THE NEWSPAPER THIS morning, I read about the death of one of the last First World War veterans. There are only three Canadians left now who fought in the Great War. William "Duke" Procter was 106 and was already famous in Canada for having gone skydiving on his one hundredth birthday. Although he broke his leg on the jump, he said he would do it again.

During the Great War, he was sixteen years old and working as a lumberjack in northern British Columbia when he enlisted. There is something thoroughly Canadian in his reason for enlisting. The obituary headline in the *Ottawa Citizen* states: GREAT WAR VETERAN SIGNED UP TO ESCAPE WINTER.

Procter probably figured the trenches of France couldn't be any worse than the snow and cold he was experiencing in the lumber camp in British Columbia. As it turned out, he never saw action but was put to work in Scotland — in a lumberyard supplying timber for trenches and tunnels.

Later in the day I visit the new Canadian War Museum in Ottawa to reflect on how war is presented and viewed at this time in Canada. There are no references to draft resisters or deserters in the museum, although I am surprised to come across a few panels that describe the widespread American resistance to the Vietnam War (it focuses mostly on the popular music of the day). In general the museum makes a genuine attempt not to glorify war but simply to present all the wars in which Canada has taken part, to thank its veterans, and to show that war is anything but glorious. Still, there is plenty of military hardware to ogle.

The visitor's guide to the museum states: "This is your museum. It is for and about people like you, ordinary Canadians who have made history. In facing extraordinary challenges, their lives shaped Canada. This is your story. It is one of fear and courage, sacrifice and survival, humanity and brutality. It is about the experience of war, and the struggle for peace, an ongoing story about a people, a country, and their place in the world." Draft resistance and the arrival of tens of thousands of draft-age Americans as immigrants in Canada were certainly aspects of "the struggle for peace," but that story remains untold here.

As I wander through the massive new museum, I view and read many of the hundreds of graphic panels on war and pass along the rows of tanks and jeeps in the vast LeBreton Gallery as if they are lined up in the hold of a supply ship heading for Liverpool. But my real reason for coming to the museum is to see Memorial Hall, a small room that has been set aside "for quiet remembrance of the sacrifices made by those who have served Canada."

After a bit of difficulty finding it, I enter Memorial Hall by walking down a long, narrow stone corridor that leads to two connected rooms. The first is a tiny space that contains five small monuments to individual Canadian peacekeepers who were killed in the line of duty. The monuments look like simple gravestones set at the edge of a field.

Next to the peacekeepers' room is a larger space, about the size of a living room in a modern ranch-style suburban home, empty but for the tomb of the Unknown Soldier, which is a simple grey-white slab mounted on the wall. Every November 11 at eleven o'clock a high window admits sunlight that falls on the tomb.

Even though the rest of the museum is crowded with visitors today, Memorial Hall, with its walls of grey stone, remains completely empty. I sit in silence on a stone bench for fifteen minutes, and not one other person enters.

It seems that the architect and designers have hidden this room away, have purposely made it difficult to find. At first I wonder why, but then I realize that this approach, in its quiet way, is quintessentially Canadian. We are not here to celebrate the glory of war. We are here to remember, to recollect, to give thanks to those who gave their lives, who sacrificed their youth, and perhaps their health; to hope beyond hope, despite all the thousands of lives lost and all the years of suffering, that somehow we human beings can stop doing this to ourselves and one another over and over again.

Epilogue

THIRTY YEARS AFTER MY time at the Farm, my wife, Faith, and I attend a *méchoui*, a gathering of current and former Farm residents and friends. On a sunny summer afternoon, we arrive at Jochen and Monik's house, which stands high on a sandy hill overlooking the fields. Across the fields can be seen the shiny metal-roofed barn that is still used as a workshop. Next to the barn are the remains of a huge root cellar dug into the side of a hill where we used to joke we would all go to live when nuclear Armageddon arrived. We fantasized about putting on puppet plays to pass the time, stealing out at night to pick turnips from the fields, and getting drunk on our own homemade turnip wine, if such a thing exists.

Vehicles and campers are parked in rows at the edge of the field where a few people toss Frisbees as several manic dogs give chase. Someone is trying to get a softball game started. A few of the people still have long hair, but not many. Some of the men have hardly any hair at all. Jochen, now grey-haired like me, greets us, then hurries off to check the lamb he's roasting. In the yard next to the house, a whole lamb turns on a spit, and long tables are set up where bowls and plates of vegetables and dips, chili, cold pastas, salads, and desserts are already being put out.

Four steps from the roasting lamb, Jochen and his German friend, Axel, have constructed a homemade hot tub. The inside of the rectangular tub is covered with part of a discarded liner from a suburban pool, and clamps hold the wooden sides together. The water in the hot tub is heated by pumping it through an old radiator, also scavenged from a house in the city, that they have placed on its side on the fire where the lamb is roasting. It's a fascinating mix: the pure funk of hippiedom joined to German engineering ingenuity.

The crowd is gathering. There's Steve, already compulsively fingering the flute in his hand, and Paul, who greets me, looking youthful as ever, a young girlfriend in tow. Lean, and always a bit tense in a crowd, Dave nods hello and turns away, and Val delivers one of her slightly mocking quips in an English accent. There's Fritz, and his partner, Kerstin, conversing in German with another visitor from the homeland. Dozens of other friends and relatives mill about drinking beer or wine and starting to snack.

Among the crowd are friends of the Farm from Wolf Lake, Wakefield, and Ottawa; Québécois relations of Monik; and the remaining eight or so residents of the Farm. Old friend Murray arrives, making puns in four languages. "Lord Lift-Off," he says. "Ouadda Seine." Heads turn. No one is sure what they have heard, not realizing that he's just combined Hebrew, French, and English, and perhaps a little Arabic. Then a grinning Wolfgang, who lived for a year in my cabin after I left the Farm, climbs the hill with four children hanging on to his long legs. There's Colleen, and Tom lugging his banjo, and Guy and Denise talking about the "hot" topic of the day — uranium mining in the region. There are little kids, half-grown kids, and full-grown kids, including Adam and Sarah, Dave and Val's children, and Jochen and Monik's younger son, Amik. Half a dozen dogs, of various sizes and makes, are getting acquainted or reacquainted, while the household cats are keeping a low profile. Someone spots a high, circling hawk and points.

Suddenly, a small red car zips into the field and parks. Out pops a woman with straight blond hair who stands in the field madly waving at the people on the hillside.

Someone shouts, "My God, it's Shirley!"

Heads in the crowd turn to look, and a small greeting party surges down the hill to exchange hugs.

Typical of Shirley, she has arrived unexpectedly, without warning, having taken the red-eye, all-night flight from Vancouver, rented a car at the Ottawa airport, and leaned on the gas pedal all the way to get here.

"How did you even know about the gathering?" I ask her.

Val explains. "I called her. She said she doubted she could make it, so I never thought to mention it."

Epilogue

"How long are you in Ottawa?" I ask.

"Just for the evening," Shirley says. "I need to be back on the set tomorrow. We're shooting *The X-Files*."

Jochen raises his beer bottle: "Now the party can really begin!"

The sun descends, and the volume of music builds as other musicians — guitarists and drummers — arrive. The scent of roasting lamb fills the air. Over a hundred people are milling about, drinking beer or wine, catching up on the lost years, sitting at the picnic table in the yard, or rocking on the four-person swing under an apple tree. Yan, Jochen's eldest son, lights the already laid bonfire, and a handful of people settle onto makeshift benches and logs set up around the firepit. Wolfgang's youngest keeps poking the fire with a stick as if he's trying to wake it up.

After everyone has eaten their fill, Val calls everyone around and announces, "Since this is the thirtieth anniversary of our arrival here at the Farm, I wanted to read you something." She begins, her voice clear and still tinged with an Oxfordshire accent. "Thirty years ago it was just an old cart track with grass growing down the middle. Coming along it about a mile, the first thing you saw was an ancient log cabin standing in an overgrown field. Inside was Mark hunkered down reading the dictionary and living on lentils ..."

By the time Val finishes her reading twenty minutes later, dusk is filtering in, drifting down from the trees. Darkness falls, and a full moon rises over the fields to the west, shiny and smooth as a drumhead. Cool, sweet moisture breathes out of the tall grass. I walk out into the field alone. For a moment I can hear, echoing faintly from the hills, the heartbeat of the earth. From the house behind me, lights and voices are blazing, but out here all has turned to blackness and silence. As it was once long ago. As it shall be again.

In the autumn of 1979, I left the Farm and moved into Ottawa with my first wife, Janet. Although I had no desire to abandon the Farm at the time, I did so at her urging in an ill-conceived attempt to save our marriage. We were separated within a few weeks of arrival in the city, and

I was living an entirely new existence, re-energized, surprisingly happy that I had given up life at the Farm.

My first apprenticeship as a writer was done. Ten years was time enough to teach myself, with the assistance of various masters, something of the art of writing, although, one wonders if this work is ever done and, in a sense, one hopes it isn't.

Turning from the computer to gaze out the window of my office at home in Ottawa, I watch the snow fall, just as I sat in the cabin at the Farm thirty winters ago, watching the drifts pile up higher and higher, collecting on the ground like the years themselves. I get up to the Farm once in a while to visit old friends who still live there, and when I walk the land, the memories in those fields lie deep.

A gust of wind arises and the snow swirls and leaps through the air like energetic snow lions at play. In time it will settle on the ground and another year will have gone by.

Selected Sources

Books

Antin, Mary. *The Promised Land*. Boston: Houghton Mifflin, 1912.
Armstrong, Karen. *A Short History of Myth*. Toronto: Alfred A. Knopf, 2005.
Aviel, Tils. *The Rarity of Flight and Secret Memories of the Future*. Venice, CA: Stone Maze Press, 2003.
Barthes, Roland. *Mythologies*. New York: Hill and Wang, 1972.
Birmingham, Stephen. *The Rest of Us: The Rise of America's Eastern European Jews*. New York: Little, Brown, 1984.
"Botha or Bourassa?" Editorial. Toronto *Globe*, March 30, 1918.
Bourassa, Henri. "Choosing Neutrality for Canada," from *What Do We Owe England?* Montreal, 1915.
Brand, Stewart. *Whole Earth Catalog*. Menlo Park, CA: Portola Institute, 1969.
Campbell, Jennifer. Obituary: "William 'Duke' Procter." *Ottawa Citizen*, December 15, 2005.
Chagall, Marc. *Chagall by Chagall*. New York: Harry N. Abrams, 1979.
_____. *My Life*. New York: Orion Press, 1960.
Cirlot, J.E. *A Dictionary of Symbols*. New York: Dorset Press, 1971.
De Ségur, Count Philippe-Paul. *Napoleon's Russian Campaign*. Trans. J.D. Townsend. New York: Time-Life Books, 1965.
Domnitch, Larry. *The Cantonist: The Jewish Children's Army of the Tsar*. Jerusalem/New York: Devora Publishing, 2003.
Fowke, Edith. *Folktales of French Canada*. Toronto: NC Press, 1979.
Fulford, Robert. "Vietnam War Resisters in Canada." *National Post*, Toronto, June 26, 2001.

Gilbert, Gustave. *Nuremberg Diary*. New York: Da Capo Press, 1995.

Hagan, John. *Northern Passage: American Vietnam War Resisters in Canada*. Cambridge, MA: Harvard University Press, 2001.

His Holiness the Dalai Lama's Views on War and Iraq Conflict. Dharmsala, India: Department of Information and International Relations, Central Tibetan Administration, March 11, 2003.

Homer. *The Iliad*. Trans. E.V. Rieu. Harmondsworth, Eng.: Penguin Books, 1950.

———. *The Iliad and the Odyssey*. Adapted by Jane Werner Watson. New York: Simon and Schuster, 1956.

Hosie, R.C. *Native Trees of Canada*. Ottawa: Environment Canada Forestry Service, 1973.

Howe, Irving. *World of Our Fathers: The Journey of the East European Jews to America and the Life They Found and Made*. New York: Harcourt Brace Jovanovich, 1976.

Hughes, Janice M. *The ROM Field Guide to Birds of Ontario*. Toronto: Royal Ontario Museum/McClelland & Stewart, 2001.

Kafka, Franz. *Selected Short Stories of Franz Kafka*. Trans. Willa and Edwin Muir. New York: The Modern Library, 1952.

Lampman, Archibald. *Lyrics of Earth*. Boston: Copeland and Day, 1895.

Levite, Alter, ed. *A Yizkor Book to Riteve: A Jewish Shtetl in Lithuania*. Cape Town: Kaplan-Kushlick Foundation, 2000.

Lin, Maya. "Making the Memorial." *New York Review of Books*, November 2, 2000.

Markel, Howard. *Quarantine! East European Jewish Immigrants and the New York City Epidemics of 1892*. Baltimore: The Johns Hopkins University Press, 1997.

Márquez, Gabriel García. *Living to Tell the Tale*. Trans. Edith Grossman. New York: Alfred A. Knopf, 2003.

McKay, Don. *Vis à Vis, Field Notes on Poetry & Wilderness*. Wolfville, NS: Gaspereau Press, 2001.

Melville, Herman. *Moby-Dick, or the Whale*. London: Richard Bentley, 1851.

Memories of a Cleveland Childhood (as spoken by Reynold Joseph

Frutkin to Ann and Bud Frutkin). Monograph, 2002.
Minard, Charles-Joseph. *Napoleon's March to Moscow: The War of 1812*. Map. Paris, 1861.
Partridge, Eric. *Origins: A Short Etymological Dictionary of Modern English*. New York: Macmillan, 1958.
Robertson, Constance Noyes. *Oneida Community: An Autobiography 1851–1876*. Syracuse, NY: Syracuse University Press, 1970.
Rombauer, Irma, and Marion Rombauer Becker. *Joy of Cooking*. New York: Bobbs-Merrill, 1975.
Rutherford, Leo. *Principles of Shamanism*. London: Thorsons, 1996.
Schama, Simon. *Landscape and Memory*. New York: Alfred A. Knopf, 1995.
Stacey, C.P. *The Military Problems of Canada*. Toronto: Ryerson Press, 1940.
Suzuki, Shunryu. *Zen Mind, Beginner's Mind*. New York: Weatherhill, 1970.
Thoreau, Henry David. *The Maine Woods*. Topeka, KS: Tandem Library Books, 1988.
_____. *Walden, or Life in the Woods*. Boston: Houghton Mifflin, 1893.
Trungpa, Chögyam. "Conquering Fear." *Shambhala Sun*, March 2002.
Vollmann, William T. *Rising Up and Rising Down*. San Francisco: McSweeney's Books, 2003.
Wilkins, Val. *This Was How I Saw It*. Monograph (undated).
Zborowski, Mark, and Elizabeth Herzog. *Life Is with People: The Culture of the Shtetl*. New York: Schocken Books, 1952.

Web Sources

"Ancient and Modern Maya Lin": *www.earlywomenmasters.net*.
"Draft Evaders: *Borisov uyezd*," December 27, 1880; "Minsk Gubernya Draft Notice," August 1876: *www.jewishgen.org*.
Durflinger, Dr. Serge. "Military History — Dispatches: Backgrounders in Canadian Military History"; "Les Purs Canayens: French Canada and Recruitment During the First World War": *www.warmuseum.ca*.

Goldstein, Jenny. "Transcending Boundaries": *www.bc.edu/bc_research*.
"Information on Particulars of Records and Attestation Papers for Canadian Soldiers in World War I and II": *http://data2.collectionscanada.ca*.
Leeson, Dan. "Military Conscription in Russia in the 19th Century": *www.JewishGen.org/infofiles*.
Mager, Andy. "We Ain't Marching Anymore: Draft and Military Resistance to the Vietnam War," *Nonviolent Activist Magazine*: *www.warresisters.org/nva*.
Mott, Jeremy. "From Protest to Resistance: The Quaker Peace Testimony During the Vietnam War," July 18, 1998: *www.quaker.org/quest/mott-vietnam01.htm*.
Ostrow, Joanne. "Photos of Coffins Draped in Evasion," April 29, 2004: *www.denverpost.com*.
Ross, Michael Alan. "The Shuls and Heders of Boston's North End": *www.angelfire.com*.
Selective Service System. "History and Records: The Vietnam Lotteries": *www.sss.gov*.
"The Vietnam Veterans Memorial Wall Page": *http://thewall-usa.com*.
"The Virtual Jewish History Tour — Cleveland": *www.jewishvirtuallibrary.org*.
Toby, H.J. "A Difference in Perspective": *www.around.ntl.sympatico.ca*.
"Vietnam Veterans Memorial": *www.nps.gov/vive/legacy*.

Photo by Sandra Russell

MARK FRUTKIN is the author of seven works of fiction, including *Fabrizio's Return*, which won the Trillium Award in 2006 and the Sunburst Award in 2007, and was shortlisted for the Commonwealth Book Regional Prize. His 1988 novel *Atmospheres Apollinaire* (available from Dundurn) was shortlisted for the Governor General's Literary Award and the Trillium. His work has been published in the United States, the United Kingdom, Russia, Poland, Spain, Holland, India, and South Korea. Frutkin lives in Ottawa.

His website is *www.markfrutkin.com*.

www.ingramcontent.com/pod-product-compliance
Lightning Source LLC
Chambersburg PA
CBHW032040150426
43194CB00006B/362